The White Lions of Timbavati

Chris McBride

The White Lions of Timbavati

PADDINGTON
PRESS LTD

NEW YORK & LONDON

Library of Congress Cataloging in Publication Data

McBride, Chris, 1941-
   The white lions of Timbavati.

    1. Lions. 2. Mammals—South Africa—Timbavati
Game Reserve. 3. Timbavati Game Reserve, South
Africa. I. Title.
QL737.C23M3   599'.74428   77-4896
ISBN 0-448-22677-4

Published by Paddington Press Ltd. in association with
Bantam Books and Ernest Stanton (Publishers) (Pty) Ltd.

Filmset by SX Composing, Leigh-on-Sea, England
Color separations by Photoprint Plates, Rayleigh, England
Text and illustrations printed and bound in Great Britain by
Jarrold & Sons Ltd.
Designed by Richard Johnson

Most of the photographs in this book were taken by Chris McBride.
Other pictures are by Mike Holmes, Tony Gray, Dr. Joseph Zamboni,
André Hugo and Tim Hancock. The illustrations on pages 78 and
194 are by Keith Joubert.

IN THE UNITED STATES
PADDINGTON PRESS LTD.
Distributed by
GROSSET & DUNLAP

IN THE UNITED KINGDOM
PADDINGTON PRESS LTD.

IN CANADA
Distributed by
RANDOM HOUSE OF CANADA LTD.

For Charlotte and Tabitha,
who share my interest in lions and
my passion for the bush;
and for my father,
who sparked this passion in me
when I was a child at Timbavati.

Contents

Acknowledgments

I WOULD LIKE TO THANK my father, Cyril McBride, who
provided me with the use of his farm at Timbavati while I
was studying my lions. Also the other landowners upon whose
property my pride ranged: Dr. Pierre Hugo, Nick Hancock,
Richard Fuld, Ludwig Whipplinger, Fanie Nel, André
Marais and Robert McBride.

My thanks also to my friends Dick Garstang, Keith
Joubert, Trygve Cooper, Arend Lambrechts and Petri
Viljoen, for their help in ways too numerous to mention. Also
to Mr. C. van Rensburg of Barclays Bank for granting me a
research loan.

I am perhaps most deeply indebted to my adviser at
Humboldt State University in Arcata, California, Professor
Archie S. Mossman; also to other members of the staff there,
notably Drs. David Kitchen, Richard Botzler and Dennis
Anderson.

My gratitude also extends to Mike Holmes for offering me his invaluable advice on photography; and to Paul Davies, who lent me the lens with which I've taken my best slides. A special thanks to Tony Gray, who helped me to put the book together in its present form; and to Diane Flanel, my editor at Paddington Press.

Finally, none of this would have been possible without the relentless assistance of my wife Charlotte, who took on all sorts of jobs both in America and Africa to support the three of us while I was at university and later studying lions in the field. She was not only invaluable in tracking and locating the lions for me, but in tolerating – even enjoying – what must have been a spectacularly unluxurious married life to date.

Preface

CATS COME IN ALL COLORS. Black, white, gray, tortoise-shell, marmalade, striped, spotted. For the domestic ones, camouflage is no problem. Their food comes to them fairly regularly, out of a can. For the wild ones, color is all important.

Leopards live in a landscape that is speckled with the shadows of leaves, and so they are spotted. Tigers spend much of their time in the long grass, stalking their prey, and so they have developed a camouflage of stripes.

And the lion, traditionally king of the beasts, is tawny, to match the dry, dusty earth of the African veld and to blend in with the short, dry grass in which it so often hunts.

Lions have to be camouflaged in this way because most of their prey can travel far faster than they can. Lions are capable of quite terrifying turns of speed, but only in short bursts. They're sprinters rather than long-distance runners, so they have to seize their prey before it's had time to get into the right gear.

Giraffes are camouflaged, too, with great patches of burnt umber on their shoulders and haunches, so that they can melt inconspicuously into the trees among which they so often congregate.

Generally, you don't see giraffes looking at lions. It's not that they're not wary of them or inquisitive. It's just that it's very difficult to spot a lion lying down in the dry grass or stretched out on the golden, sandy earth under a shingayi tree.

But recently in a private game reserve called Timbavati, adjoining the Kruger National Park in the Transvaal in South Africa, the giraffes have been spending a lot of time staring at a few select lion cubs – cubs that are very different, and a lot easier to see.

They are, in fact, white. As white as polar bears. Not albinos but normal, healthy lions – the first truly white lions the world has ever known.

There's an albino lion in the Kruger National Park. Albinos appear to be white, but this is due to their abnormal, total lack of pigmentation, which also affects the color of the eyes. The white lions of Timbavati, however, are positively white-pigmented with normal, yellow eyes, only a shade or so lighter than the golden yellow of their mother's eyes.

There was a white lion born in a game park in Florida some years ago, but it turned tawny after a year. The Timbavati cubs – Temba and Tombi, as they came to be called – are almost two years old now and they are still unmistakably white.

Chris McBride discovered the white lions while he was living in Timbavati with his wife Charlotte and his daughter Tabitha, who was four at the time. He had been studying the pride into which these cubs were born as part of the fieldwork requirement for his master's degree in wildlife management. This involved his walking about a thousand miles through lion country, observing the lions in minute detail and photographing them in their most intimate moments.

These moments included the mating of Agamemnon, one of the pride males, with Tabby, a pride lioness – the mating that almost undoubtedly resulted in the conception of the white cubs, born in October 1975.

The fact that Tabby's cubs turned out to be white was, at the time, extraneous to McBride's academic work. But as he watched them grow, they became his prime concern.

Their color may make them too conspicuous to hunt successfully by night or day. So far they don't appear to have been victimized by the other lions in any way because of their color. But what will happen to them if they leave the pride? Will they be in danger from other tawny-colored lions? Are they likely to attract the attention of big game hunters if they leave the safety of the reserve? Or will they simply starve to death because, without camouflage, they may not be able to hunt?

There have been rumors and legends of white lions in Africa for centuries. It is certainly possible that white cubs were born here in the past and simply disappeared before anyone caught a glimpse of them. In view of the high mortality rate among lion cubs and the fact that a white cub would be that much more vulnerable, the chances that a white lion cub could be born and die unseen in this largely uninhabited area are very high. In the wild, after the event, you never know what has happened. With vultures, hyenas and other scavengers around, all the evidence is destroyed.

This time, however, if something happens to the white cubs and they fail to survive, we at least have proof that they existed as seen in the photographs in this book. The case of the white lions of Timbavati is here fully documented.

But this is far more than the story of Temba and Tombi and the other members of their pride. Partly as a result of McBride's studies in wildlife management, and partly as a result of all the hundreds of hours he has spent walking around this primitive wilderness, he has become deeply involved with ecology. His experiences have contributed to his acute awareness of the delicate balance that nature has achieved over the millennia to enable this totally un-spoiled tract of land to support such a staggering variety of wildlife.

In this extraordinary place, an oasis in a world of dis-appearing and endangered species, what appears to be a new strain has suddenly emerged. And for once man, responsible for the destruction of so much wildlife, is in a position to use a whole battery of new and sophisticated techniques to foster these unique cubs.

At least they were unique.

Until one day, in August 1976, when McBride discovered another pure white lion cub, born to a different lioness. This raises the intriguing possibility that yet more white cubs may be born, and with man's help may be enabled to survive.

So it looks as if the story of the white lions of Timbavati is only just beginning.

PADDINGTON PRESS
London, 1977

CHAPTER ONE

Two Families in the Lowveld

THE BEGINNING OF OCTOBER in the Lowveld of the northeastern Transvaal is the end of the dry season. Here and there the stirring of spring brings fresh leaves and blossoms, but most of the trees are still bare and the grass is as pale as straw. No soaking rains have fallen for months and rivers like the Machaton have slumbered dryly through a Southern Hemisphere winter of relatively cool blue days and sharp, starry nights – dryly, it must be said, for the rivers are waterless, sandy spruits, or beds, for three hundred days every year. When the rains come in early December, rivers like the Machaton become brief torrents eight to ten feet deep before they are swallowed up again by the thirsty soil.

The deep sandy riverbed of the Machaton (pronounced Ma-chát-un) snakes through the Lowveld only a few miles from the western boundary of the huge Kruger National Park, some 350 miles northeast of Johannesburg, and is itself within a private nature reserve. The reserve was formed in 1955 when twenty-eight local landowners agreed to dedicate themselves to preserving and fostering the wealth of wildlife on their lands by combining their holdings. They called it the Timbavati Nature Reserve and adopted as their motto the words of King George VI of England:

> The wildlife of today is not ours to dispose of as we please. We have it in trust. We must account for it to those who come after.

Timbavati is a unique place, part of a very ancient shield of land which has been subjected to almost no geological changes – no volcanic eruptions, no ice age and no glaciers – and few man-made changes. It is 208 square miles of virgin bush. There are no internal fences and the individual parcels of land within it – there are now fifteen – are marked only by tracks cut through the bush, so that the wildlife is free to wander from farm to farm.

The word *farm* is a misnomer perhaps, because the land is not cultivated in any way and never has been since the beginning of time. Timbavati's farms are simply tracts of wild bush supporting a bewildering variety of animal life ranging in size from elephants to mosquitoes. At first the farms were used as hunting grounds and country retreats where the owners and their guests could find peace and quiet away from their professional lives, but the farms are now dedicated principally to the conservation of wildlife.

The area is called Timbavati after a river which flows through the southern part of the reserve. Flows, again, is not quite the right word, because for most of the year the Timbavati, like the Machaton, is a wide expanse of soft sand.

16

Paradoxically, though, Timbavati means "the river that never dries out" – and this is true to the extent that you can always find a few pools here and there along its length.

This is primeval land, untouched by man since the first days of the world. There's only one public road in the whole area, cutting through a tiny segment of the reserve to the Orpen Gate of the Kruger National Park, and that is soon going to be replaced by a road right around the perimeter; so it's truly the wild.

Apart from the fifteen current owners, who are not permanent residents and visit the area only occasionally, Timbavati is inhabited on a full-time basis by only the game warden and his family, the people who staff the two commercial game-viewing lodges, a few officials of the Department of Nature Conservation and about three hundred Shangaans, scattered in small encampments throughout the reserve.

At the last count, the population of Timbavati also included 13,000 impala, 2,800 wildebeest, 1,400 zebra, 1,050 giraffe, 500 kudu, 450 buffalo, 70 elephant, 300 waterbuck, lots of warthog and duiker, vervet monkeys and baboons, and the predators – about 150 lions, 200 hyenas, 100 leopards, 80 or more cheetahs, as well as polecats, jackal, mongoose, honey badger, eagles, vultures. And that's only the beginning of the catalog.

This is the Lowveld. To the newcomer, it looks flat and featureless. Everything about it is low. It's all lower than two thousand feet above sea level, and most of it is far lower than that. The trees look stunted. Some have simply died of old age and stand there, gaunt and bleached by the scorching sun. Others have been pushed over or uprooted by elephants, who eat the leaves and roots as well as the bark.

With all these shattered trees and the whitened skeletons

left over from the predators' kills, there are those who say that the place looks like a World War I battlefield. But people who have learned to appreciate its vast, obsessively peaceful, brooding silence return to it again and again; and they are never very happy too far away from it.

"But even greater than its wonderful fauna, its subtropical flora, its unrivaled scenery," wrote Jan Smuts, South Africa's most famous premier, "is the mysterious, eerie spirit which broods over this vast solitude, where no human pressure is felt, where the human element itself shrinks into utter insignificance, and where a subtle spirit, much older than the human spirit, grips you and makes you one with itself. To those who wish to experience a thrill which is unlike any they have experienced before, I venture to recommend a visit to this home of the Earth Spirit. . . ."

Beauty is a difficult word to use because it means so many things to so many people, but to me the Lowveld – and specifically Timbavati – is unquestionably one of the most serenely beautiful places in the world.

All of the fifteen farms in the Timbavati reserve have their own bush camps. Most of them are composed of a cluster of rondavels (pronounced ron-dá-vels), circular mud and wattle structures, with a conical roof thatched with reeds. Based on traditional African design, they not only look right for the surroundings but are also extremely practical. They're relatively inexpensive to build, and because of the insulating properties of the thatch they keep cool in the hot, humid weather and yet prove surprisingly warm when it is chilly.

There are, of course, a few more imposing residences, bright with bougainvillaea and other exotic plants, but the

18

basic pattern is absolute simplicity: no electricity or other amenities, and sanitation is usually in the form of what is known as "the long drop." Most of the vehicles used in these camps are of the land rover/jeep variety equipped with four-wheel drive to enable them to traverse the often trackless bush and churn their way through the soft sand of the innumerable riverbed crossings.

My father and his brother joined together thirty years ago and bought nearly ten thousand acres of the bush here, when it was worth less than three dollars an acre. It is right through my father's holding that the Machaton riverbed runs.

His farm is called Vlakgesicht (pronounced Flóck-ga-zigt). It is commonly known as Vlak – the word simply means "flat view" – and it is typical of the rough accommodations in the area. The main building, which has two bedrooms, a kitchen and bathroom, is normally reserved for guests: It is flanked by two rondavels. One is used as a lounge, dining room and study; the other is a bedroom. Finally, there's the *guma*, a circular enclosure of reeds, more than twelve feet high, which serves as a windbreak when we decide to eat out of doors around a *braai*, or barbecue.

Early in 1975 my father offered me his camp as a base from which to study the lions. And so we moved in: my wife Charlotte, my daughter Tabitha (more often known as Tabs), and I.

We had neither electricity nor telephone. Kerosene (paraffin) lamps and candles provided all the light we ever needed and an old kerosene refrigerator chilled our perishables . . . whenever it was working.

We didn't really miss the telephone. In fact, isolation seemed only to strengthen our bond with the bush. When there was no way to avoid making a telephone call, we'd simply hop in the jeep and drive to one of the few places in the reserve equipped with a phone: the warden's house, thirty minutes away; a game-viewing lodge called Sohebele, almost an hour away; or Dr. Pierre Hugo's adjoining farm, which was on the main road and had a bush telephone in a box beside a tree, three-quarters of an hour away. These phones were all connected to an open party line, linked to the outside world – intermittently, and usually reluctantly – through the exchange in Hoedspruit, regional center of the area, about forty miles away.

Once every few weeks we went into Hoedspruit for mail, food and other supplies. There was also an open market at Acornhoek, a bit further away, where we occasionally went for fresh rations of fruit and vegetables. We never bothered much about newspapers and we didn't even have a radio at the camp.

We were at Timbavati for one purpose only: to look at lions. I've always been fascinated by lions. It's a very common fascination – the appeal of the earth's ultimate predator, if you exclude mankind. But there's a lot more to it than that. I suppose because of its size and incredible strength and utter ruthlessness, the male lion holds an unassailable position as a symbol of total power.

I was enrolled in a course in wildlife management at Humboldt State University in Arcata, California, and in order to get my master's degree I needed to spend some months in the field working on my thesis. I knew that a year was too short a time in which to research and write a thesis on lions in general – it would obviously be superficial; so I decided instead to study one particular pride in depth.

Even before I finally got down to work, I knew that I was going to have to spend a lot of my time just hanging around, watching. Watching and waiting and listening.

It's the only possible way you can learn about lions.

I planned to observe their courting, mating and breeding habits, the frequency and nature of their kills, their use of the terrain, their routes; I was even planning to go into such details as their panting rates at different times of the day and in different temperatures, and I aimed to keep a record of their roaring patterns in order to build up as complete a picture as possible of one pride of lions in the wild.

When I moved to Vlak I didn't have any particular pride in mind. I didn't even know if there was a resident pride of lions in the vicinity of the Machaton. But I did know that there were lions down there. My father, after all, had been seeing them there for thirty years. So I decided to start from that point and find out for myself if there was a resident pride, and if so, to get acquainted with it as rapidly as possible.

It isn't very easy to identify all the members of a pride initially, because they tend to break up at certain times into subgroups — partly to protect the cubs, and partly because a subgroup is a more efficient hunting unit. The only way you can recognize members of the same pride is by the way they greet each other by rubbing cheeks, and by the absence of any excessively aggressive tendencies, unless they are on a kill.

For the first three months at Vlak, I walked the territory hour after hour after hour, about a thousand miles in all, usually with an experienced African tracker. Charlotte, Tabs and I also spent a good deal of time driving around the bush in a jeep, trying to get the animals conditioned to the sound and smell and sight of the vehicle.

We did this for a very simple reason. You can find lions

on foot – it's probably the best way to go after them – but if they spot you or get your scent, they usually move away immediately. Once they become accustomed to a vehicle, however, which takes about three months, they ignore it completely and behave perfectly naturally. It could be that the smell of gasoline and oil and rubber are so strong that they can't scent the humans inside and therefore don't associate the vehicles with man. We developed a routine of discovering where the lions were by walking through the bush and following the spoor (or tracks). When we found them, as often as not asleep, we would retrace our steps, return in the jeep and watch them for hours, gradually acquainting ourselves with them and getting them accustomed to our presence.

In this way I gradually sorted out the Machaton pride of lions from all the others in the area, and came to know them amazingly well.

As we listened to the sounds of the bush at night from our rondavel, we eventually learned to distinguish the roars of our own lions from those of adjoining prides. Charlotte, who is far better at identifying animals than I am, could even tell the individual lions apart. Her knowledge of the bush is quite uncanny.

Even Tabs, scarcely four, soon became adept at spotting lion spoor on our frequent drives through the bush and never fell into the common trap of confusing their spoor with those of the hyena.

So, all in all, it was very much a family affair – both on our part and on the part of the lions we had begun to study.

The pride of lions that roams the bush along the Machaton

is led by two magnificent males known as Achilles and Agamemnon. Between them they share half a dozen lionesses. We soon had names for all the members of the pride. The six lionesses we called Golden, Dimples, Scarleg, Greta, Lona, and Tabby, soon to be the mother of a very special litter. Then there were Golden's three "teenage" males, the Three Musketeers, and their sister Suzie Wong.

As we observed them at all hours of the day and night, and as the patterns of their life began to emerge, we found it a highly organized arrangement.

The two male lions seem immensely proud, to the point of arrogance, and yet they are intensely loyal to each other. Both of them mate with all six lionesses, and apparently without the faintest hint of jealousy. It's an arrangement that works out very much in the lions' favor.

Almost invariably, it is the lionesses of the pride who do what might be called the "family hunting." They are far better equipped for it than the males because they are lighter and much more agile. The resultant feast — be it wildebeest, impala, warthog or giraffe — is served in a very strict order, particularly in times of stress, when food is scarce: first the two big males; then the lionesses themselves; then the juniors of the pride; and finally the cubs, if any, who have to take their chances. There's no sentiment about seeing that the youngest or weakest member of the brood gets a fair share. In the bush, the weakest simply go without.

When they're not out hunting for the pride or caring for their young, the lionesses are available for mating. Available is an understatement. According to lion expert George Schaller, a mating bout between two lions can last for as long as two days and involve as many as one hundred and fifty couplings. Lions, incidentally, have no fixed mating season because lionesses are polyestrous – they can come into heat at any time.

In return Achilles and Agamemnon make their own special contribution to the pride. I've noticed that the two lions often go off together, and it appears from these ramblings that they cover every part of the pride's range. In a single night I've heard them roaring from a dozen different directions. And by day I've often seen them marking out the pride's range by squirting a glandular secretion on trees and shrubs. In this way they are serving notice in their range and to all nomad lions and males from adjoining prides that the Machaton is occupied territory, under a very firm system of government.

Scraping the ground with the hind foot while urinating is another of their marking methods. Lions will also frequently scratch deeply into the bark of trees. This is partly to sharpen their claws, but it might well be another method of marking. I've sometimes seen the senior lionesses, particularly Golden, marking bushes; but Achilles and Agamemnon did it twenty times as often.

If they had to, Achilles and Agamemnon would fight to defend their territory, although I've never seen it happen. (I've only once seen a lion dead as a result of a territorial fight; the death rate from fighting is extremely low.) Normally if nomads impinge on a pride area, they get a severe warning from the pride male or males, and clear off without attempting to fight. Nomads are not welcomed by any pride.

Basically the whole social cohesion, the stability of the pride, depends on the dominance of its leading males. According to Schaller, in one instance a group of nomadic males deposed the leader of a pride similar to the Machaton pride and promptly ate a number of the cubs. The pride took two years to adjust to the new regime and to resume its normal rate of cub survival.

The rest of the time, when they are not eating or mating or worrying about the defense of the range, Achilles and Agamemnon are fully occupied conserving their energy. All of the lions are great at that. Most of them spend between sixteen and twenty hours a day resting.

The dry season is a good time for the Machaton lions. The pride prefers the mild warmth of the shorter days. They shelter from the noonday sun in the umbrella-like shade of the white-thorned shingayi, a species of acacia. But they don't pant their days away as they do during the oppressive, humid heat of the summer. Often the two big males, Achilles and Agamemnon, go off together, disdaining the company of their lionesses and the younger lions who may be found alone or in groups, waiting for the dusk.

The longer nights of winter and spring also mean more time for hunting, for the Machaton lions are essentially nocturnal stalkers. The hunting is easier and better then too, as their prey is drawn by thirst to the only remaining water sources – two dams, a marsh and a perennial spring. So the chances of finding and killing are now far greater than in high summer, during the rainy season, with tall grasses and leafy bushes and pans of water at every turn. In winter the prey must turn up at one of the four predictable spots, and when they do, there is no shelter to hide them.

The pride's range is roughly oval-shaped, about six and a half miles from tip to tip, and nearly four miles across at its widest point. It varies slightly at different times of the year, and is extended by a few miles during the rainy season when the lions are forced to venture farther afield to capture their prey. It is an area of twisted trees, marula, leadwood, knobthorn and shingayi, interspersed with scrub and grassland. Even the plains are not the open plains of East Africa; visibility is seldom more than two hundred yards.

At the heart and center of the region dominated by the Machaton pride is the broad artery of the Machaton river, a five-mile stretch of it, dry as I've said for about three hundred days every year and fringed with a border of thick riverine bush with roots long enough to reach the water that lies deep beneath the dry riverbed. Beyond the riverine bush there is a belt of sandy, alkaline plain, where the most prevalent type of tree is the shingayi.

And it is here, on the banks of the Machaton, in the shade of a shingayi, that Achilles and Agamemnon and their pride are usually to be found.

And here, too, may usually be found the McBride family, watching them.

CHAPTER TWO

Encounter in the Bush

IF YOU WANT TO OBSERVE LIONS behaving naturally, there's only one way to do it: from a jeep or a land rover or some similar vehicle, properly protected, with a lion cage built around it – that is, a cage designed and constructed for the purpose of keeping lions out.

Within three months, my lions became completely accustomed to the jeep and would approach within a few feet of it, provided those of us inside sat tight and talked in whispers. They'd even come and lie down within the shade of the vehicle.

My decision to have a cage built around the jeep was dictated principally by the fact that I needed to feel fully relaxed in order to observe the lions as I planned to do. I doubt very much if that cage would have kept a really determined lioness out, but at least inside it I felt safe. I was able to watch the lions and chart their behavior in a way that I couldn't possibly have done had I been in an open car with a full-grown lioness only a few yards away.

There was another very good reason for the cage. I didn't want to have to shoot any of my lions. Without the cage that might have become necessary. If I had felt that any of us were threatened at any time, I would have had to shoot.

The cage gave us a feeling of security – largely illusory, but it worked. Looking at them through the iron bars we could accept threatening behavior, even mock charges, without overreacting and shooting at them.

In the same way, whenever I walked on foot among the lions, I always carried a gun big enough to stop a charging lion in its tracks. This particular gun would have stopped any animal; it was an elephant gun. If you carry a gun as powerful as that, you probably won't ever have to use it. The gun gives you a certain feeling of confidence, and the animals sense this. Knowing that you can stop them, you can afford to let them come at you until the very last moment. A lion is a big animal. You'd have to be a very bad shot to miss, especially if it's coming right at you, because the target is getting bigger all the time.

If you are carrying only a small rifle, that can be dangerous on a number of scores. Sensing your feeling of insecurity, a lion may well attack and you might be tempted to shoot before you really need to. Also, if you do shoot, you might not kill it instantly.

Jack Mathebula, an African tracker who lives in Timbavati, was one of my frequent companions on my walks through the bush. Jack is the best tracker I've ever come across. He has taught me most of what I know about that dangerous and imprecise art.

The first time I went tracking with Jack I was young

and rash, and we had an experience with a lioness that turned my stomach to water. It's from experiences like this that you learn exactly what you can do with lions. I still remember it vividly, though it happened more than thirteen years ago.

We were walking together near the Machaton when we found some lion tracks and drag marks. Something – obviously a kill – had been dragged down toward the river. Perhaps there was a lioness with cubs around somewhere. In the soft sand of the riverbed we saw the drag marks again and I said to Jack: "Come on, let's go through."

"No, wait," he said urgently in Zulu. Then: "Look."

I looked at the bush on the far side, and for a long time I couldn't see anything. Then I spotted it – the top of one ear.

We decided to go back to the higher ground for a better view. The previous day I'd come across twenty-five lions feeding on a giraffe and as soon as we appeared, they fled. So maybe I was feeling a bit overconfident.

From the higher position we couldn't see the lioness at all, so I decided to throw a stone into the bush to see whether she was still there.

"*Haye*. No," Jack said, and shook his head.

The stone went through a shrub and hit the ground. Nothing happened.

I threw a second . . . and there was a slight movement.

Then there was a sudden explosion. The trees just burst apart and suddenly the lioness was over the riverbed and coming straight at us. Her tail was going like a whip and all the time there was this terrifying, rumbling roar.

I had my rifle up and she was big in my sights when Jack said: "*Yima! Ungalibulali!* Stand still. Don't shoot." The lioness suddenly stopped about twenty paces away from us. There was still this low rumbling sound coming from deep within her stomach. Her tail was lashing away and the dust was flying everywhere. I kept my gun leveled on her.

Again Jack spoke quite softly but very firmly: "No. Don't shoot."

The lioness stood her ground for a few seconds. Then she backed off slowly, still growling, toward the river. Sheepishly I lowered my gun.

That lesson served me well on other occasions. One time a friend and I were out tracking, and three lionesses came at us, straight out of the riverine bush – all at once and at full speed. It was a terrifying predicament. When they stopped about twenty-five paces from us, we had our rifles trained on them. We stood our ground, and remembering Jack's confidence on the previous occasion, I held my fire. Eventually a kind of guarded, mutual respect was established, and this time we were able to back away, reasonably confident that the lions wouldn't charge again.

Jack was equally insistent on driving home the point that if you did turn and run, you'd be dead within seconds. I've yet to try this one out, for obvious reasons.

In all the time I've been tracking lions, I've been charged six times – always by a lioness, I might add, and probably because there were cubs around. Thanks to Jack's counsel, though, I've never had to shoot. I'd be the last to deny that it's a completely natural reaction to fire at a charging beast, but I often wonder how many charging lions have been shot quite unnecessarily?

With that kind of experience behind me and a cage around our jeep – plus a Westley-Richards .404 rifle inside the jeep – we felt safe enough to sit for hours and hours getting acquainted with the Machaton pride.

Achilles and Agamemnon, the two pride males, are both magnificent animals, but of the two Achilles is more alert, more of a leader. When they wake up after a rest, it is always Achilles who moves off first. Agamemnon looks battle-weary; he has many scars and his left eye is slightly recessed, almost certainly the result of a fight with another lion. Achilles and Agamemnon are very close to each other. In fact, the bond between the two of them seems to be much stronger than the bond between them and the rest of the pride. They are almost always together: sometimes on their own, sometimes with one or another subgroup of the pride, or sometimes with a single lioness.

My own feeling is that they grew up in a different pride. Then, when they were between two and three years old, they were thrown out by the pride and became nomads, traveling together. What probably happened next was that they then came across the Machaton pride, threw out the pride male or males, and took it over. It seems likely that they are brothers, possibly twins, and that their period as nomads strengthened the bond between them because they would have had to hunt together as partners in order to survive. This would explain why they appear to be so much closer to one another than they are to the rest of the pride. I've never seen any sign of aggression between them, even on a kill or during a mating session.

Golden, the mother of the Three Musketeers and Suzie Wong, the pride teenagers, is very aggressive, very alert. At the time we started to observe the Machaton lions, she was the leading lioness of the pride. At various periods I've seen the other five lionesses make submissive gestures toward her. She's large for a lioness and deeply golden in color, hence her name.

31

Scarleg — obviously so called because she has a scarred leg — seems to be second in the lioness hierarchy. She's very aggressive, and has become much more so since she had a litter of her own some eight or nine months after the birth of the white cubs. She's even made mock charges at the jeep.

Tabby, named after my daughter, seems to come third in the hierarchy. She's a small lioness, probably very young, with a slight scar on the middle of her nose, which means that we can identify her instantly in a photograph. She's completely casual. Right from the beginning, she showed no fear of us or of the jeep. She usually behaved as if we weren't there at all, though on occasion she would come right up to the jeep to investigate. Tabby is completely at ease with her cubs and doesn't appear at all nervous about their well-being, even when they play beside the jeep.

Then there's Dimples, so named because she has a black mark like a dimple on one cheek. Dimples is Tabby's great friend. She was with Tabby the first time we saw the white cubs and she's been with her ever since. She hasn't had any cubs of her own during the time I've been studying the pride.

The other two lionesses are Greta and Lona (both names inspired by Greta Garbo, who always wanted to be alone). These I know only by exclusion; if it isn't any of the ones I know really well, then it's got to be one of them. They appear to be more on the outskirts of the pride than an integral part of it, and they're both very wary.

And that, the cubs apart, is the Machaton pride as we came to know it in the early months of 1975.

PREVIOUS PAGE: I tracked my lions initially by following the spoor. You can usually tell how recently the lions have passed by the extent that the spoor is eroded away.

ABOVE: Jack Mathebula is the best tracker I've ever come across. He's taught me most of what I know about that imprecise and difficult art.

RIGHT: Aniel, another of my frequent companions in the bush.

FAR RIGHT: We used the jeep because it isn't possible to observe lions closely on foot; as soon as they catch your scent they move away. We had a cage built around our jeep to give us a feeling of security.

ABOVE: Tabby, named after my daughter, is third in the lioness hierarchy of the Machaton pride. Pale in color, she's a small lioness and probably very young.

RIGHT: Agamemnon, a superb creature, unconsciously enjoying his unassailable, unmistakable virility.

LEFT: Tabby stalked up to Agamemnon and we could see at a glance that this was the beginning of a flirtation.

ABOVE: Eventually she lay down on her paws and he mounted her again and again.

OVERLEAF: What I didn't realize at the time was that the outcome of this particular mating was to be something totally unique . . .

LEFT: Lions, like most wild animals, are perfectly camouflaged – but Temba and Tombi stuck out like sore thumbs.

ABOVE: From the outset, we were worried about the survival of the white cubs. Without camouflage, young wild animals are terribly vulnerable.

OVERLEAF: Temba (right) is the Zulu word for "hope"; Tombi simply means "girl."

FOLLOWING PAGES: Their tawny brother we named Vela, meaning "surprise." We didn't reckon that he would have any problems. But if the others stayed as white as they were, how could they ever hope to hunt?

Vela was a slow developer and rather shy at first. His white brother, Temba, was completely different in temperament, constantly in trouble, and always receiving minor injuries. He wasn't so much aggressive as slaphappy.

Early in May, long before the cubs came on the scene, I was driving the battered old jeep with its lion cage through the bush. A low orange sun was burning through a stately wild fig tree that grew down by the riverbed as I pulled into a clearing. This was toward the end of my period of hoofing it all over the range to find out for myself which routes the lions were using.

I didn't know exactly what I was looking for that day, but I had a feeling. With lions it's more often a feeling than anything else. And this day I felt I was in for something special.

I watched for a while and suddenly I spotted Agamemnon coming out of the riverine bush about twenty yards away — for once without Achilles. A superb creature, unconsciously enjoying his unassailable unmistakable virility.

A few minutes later a lioness appeared. I don't like imputing human characteristics to animals, but I swear there was something almost coquettish in her lithe, supple movements. I recognized her immediately. She was one of the youngest of the six lionesses and a bit paler than all the others, the one we called Tabby.

She stalked tautly up to Agamemnon and lifted a paw to his massive head. He stood his ground. Next she withdrew a few paces, then walked briskly past his nose, rubbing herself against his mane and leaving not the slightest doubt of her intentions.

Agamemnon got the message. As the scent of the aroused female reached his nostrils, he shook his head and his scarred muzzle wrinkled back, not in a snarl but in a grimace of acknowledgment.

You could say it was the beginning of a flirtation. I didn't think for a moment that I would ever be lucky enough to see – and, with a friend, photograph – its consummation.

A few weeks later, on June 6, 1975, I was out in the bush again, bumping along in a closed Wagoneer (another jeep-type vehicle) with Joe Zamboni, an American friend who happened to be staying with us.

We saw something dart across the road a long way ahead. Thinking it might be a lion, Joe and I hopped out. We approached the spot and had just started to look for spoor, when suddenly we heard the unmistakable, intimate mutterings of lions in the bush nearby. So in we went – first me with my Westley-Richards .404, Joe right behind. But there was no sign of the lions.

Then we saw a vulture – one vulture, near Rock Spruit – and we walked over toward it. Even if it's only one vulture, it's always worth investigating, for it might indicate a kill in the vicinity. As we got closer we saw two or three more. Joe was busy photographing them when suddenly we heard a peculiar growling noise – a noise I'd never heard before in all the hours I'd spent listening to lions.

It sounded about thirty yards away, so we went very quietly and ended by walking a few hundred yards. Then we saw a big lion – it was Agamemnon again, standing in the low combretum bush. I'd recognize him instantly, anywhere. He was a long way off, and looking the other way, so we crept back to fetch the Wagoneer.

We returned to the spot in the vehicle, and there was the lion standing over a wildebeest kill. There wasn't much of the carcass left. Agamemnon had fed, and fed handsomely. Then a lioness came out of the bush. Tabby again, no possible doubt about that either. She walked straight up to Agamemnon and he started to trail her, nose to rear. Tabby kept flicking her tail. She was small, probably not much more than a teenager, so she could easily have been his daughter or grand-daughter.

Eventually she lay down on her paws and he mounted her, growling the way a lion growls only at mating and biting at the nape of her neck very softly, though with his teeth bared.

We watched them spellbound for a full two and a half hours, until it was too dark to see, or photograph, any more. They had repeated the mating ritual ten times and the sequence of actions was always the same.

What we had been witnessing and photographing was a primitive, primordial act – something that has been going on since the beginning of time. What I didn't realize then was that the outcome of this particular mating was to be something totally unique.

CHAPTER THREE

Temba and Tombi

WE FOUND THE CUBS completely by chance in early October 1975.

Well, not completely by chance. Charlotte had seen Tabby in mid-September looking extremely pregnant. Two weeks later she again spotted the lioness, looking much more slender. It seemed likely that Tabby had had her cubs, and Charlotte told us roughly where to look for her.

The weather wasn't very good that day, and as I was suffering from flu, I decided to stay in bed and read. My older sister Lan, up from Johannesburg for a visit, went off in the Wagoneer with her son James and Johnson, one of the older trackers in the area. Johnson, a Matabele, is a very rugged character. He's been known to walk all the way from his home in Plumtree, Rhodesia, to Johannesburg, a good four hundred and fifty miles, most of it through lion country. He'd walk all day and sleep up in the trees at night;

52

the journey would take him three or four weeks, but he thought nothing of it.

Hoping that Tabby had already given birth and that they might catch her in a rare moment with her new cubs, Lan, James and Johnson headed straight for the place we called the Plains, an area of sparse scrub and knobthorn trees.

As they approached the spot that Charlotte described, she suddenly braked and switched off the motor.

"Look, James, a lioness," she whispered.

"Where?" he asked, searching the terrain without any success. Lions are notoriously difficult to spot, even when you are right on top of them.

Then he saw her. It was Tabby, only about twenty-five yards from the track, under a shingayi. She lay there, quite unconcerned, looking back at the jeep. Beside her was the remains of a wildebeest kill on which she'd been feeding.

In absolute silence, Lan, James and Johnson sat and waited.

Within a minute, a little head popped up behind the lioness. To Lan's amazement, it was snow-white.

Then another little head appeared – tawny.

And yet a third – snow-white again.

Lan was staggered. She'd heard of very rare albino cubs, but these had yellow eyes – normal lions' eyes. It was quite clear that they weren't albinos. They were ordinary, seemingly healthy lions. Except that they were pure white.

She drove back to get me – "like a maniac," as she put it. She found me still in bed, reading and unable, because of the flu, to get as excited as I should have been about the news.

"Are you sure they're not just pale?" I asked her.

She was furious. "No. They're white. Pure white," she insisted.

By this time I was sufficiently interested to drag myself out of bed and grab a camera. I was only sorry that Charlotte happened to be helping out in the Sohebele game-viewing lodge, too far away to be fetched in time, because at this period she knew far more about the workings of this particular camera than I did.

So, in spite of my health and my own basic doubts about any such thing as white lions, I joined the crowd around the Wagoneer – which by this time had become quite considerable. The news about the white lions had quickly spread around the camp and a rather impressive viewing party had assembled.

There were Lan and her son James, naturally, and Johnson, who couldn't wait to have another look, and Tabs, and a sixteen-year-old African girl named Gracie who used to look after her for us, and Gracie's sister, who happened to turn up at the last minute.

The Wagoneer was as full as it's ever been.

Lan drove back to the spot where she'd seen Tabby and the cubs. They were all there, still in the same position. The cubs stayed close to their mother, but now and then we would get a glimpse of one of them over her tawny shoulder. But only a glimpse. Never once did we see all three cubs together. I worked away with the camera, as best I could.

After twenty minutes the cubs grew bolder. One by one they wandered off into the bush behind their mother. We now spotted another lioness, Dimples, lying in the nearby shade. Tabby stood up, and from the Wagoneer we could hear her calling softly to her brood. It's hard enough to indicate human accents phonetically, let alone animal cries, but it was a short, sharp sound, something like the *oo* in *book*, but higher in pitch. This was the seldom-heard sound that adult lions make when they are hunting together and want to communicate without alerting other animals. It's a sound that has evolved over the centuries, a sound which is nondirectional and doesn't seem to attract the attention of other animals.

Tabby called again – the same short, sharp *oo* sound – and yet again, a third time.

From a thicket emerged a tiny tawny form. Then two more furry shapes – white as polar bears, but unmistakably lions. It was the first time I had seen them in the open. One had broad, quizzical features, suggesting an adventurous male. This was Temba, as we came to call him: Temba, the Zulu word for "hope." The other had the triangular face of a female and was much more cautious. She became simply Tombi, which is Zulu for "girl."

Temba and Tombi ambled over to join their brother, whom we later named Vela, meaning "surprise." And there they all stood – Vela and the white lions of Timbavati – in the secure patch of Lowveld grass, listening as their mother called out to them.

Thirty yards away, Lan started the engine and we turned discreetly for home, leaving them to the wildebeest carcass that had so fortuitously pinned them to the spot.

Looking back on it later that night, I began to realize what a momentous find we had made. The reality of having discovered – no less photographed – the first truly white lions in recorded history was quite overwhelming to me.

Suddenly it also dawned on me that these extraordinary white cubs were almost certainly the result of the mating Joe

Zamboni and I had witnessed in June. And we had photographs of that as well.

I tried to reconstruct the timing. The cubs were roughly two weeks old when we saw them, and knowing that the gestation period of lions is between 106 and 110 days, there wasn't much doubt that what we had seen and photographed on June 6 had resulted in the birth of these white cubs.

Apart from the fact that I was sure at the time that I had correctly identified Agamemnon and Tabby, there was now plenty of documentary evidence. Joe's pictures showed Agamemnon with his clearly recessed eye; and Tabby was equally easy to identify in the photographs from the small scar on her nose.

Even then, as early as that, I began to wonder what we should do about these white cubs. I felt a very special sense of responsibility for their survival.

Obviously there would be zoos, and probably circuses, all over the world that would be interested. A white lion would be an undeniable attraction. But my first instinct was to keep them in the wild and see what would happen, whatever the risk. The casualty rate among lions cubs in the wild is as high as seventy percent, so realistically what chance had these cubs?

And yet I was determined, initially at least, to let them stand up to the odds.

The morning after her momentous find, Lan took the Wagoneer out to the Plains again; she was convinced that the lions would still be there. Unfortunately, I was still feeling ill, too ill to accompany her – much to my disappointment.

One of the endless fascinations of the bush is the way it constantly springs surprises on you and forces you to stop and take a look. This time for Lan, an avid birdwatcher, it was a pair of hornbills, bobbing and bowing in a comical mating display. With yellow scimitar beaks almost as big as their puny black-and-white bodies, they proved an irresistible distraction and she stopped to watch.

But the thought of the white lion cubs soon got her going again, and she even managed to resist the temptation to pause and watch a herd of blue wildebeest and two zebras with young foals.

She got to the Plains as quickly as she could, and there they were, exactly as they had been the previous day – Tabby and her fabulous cubs.

Lan parked under a leadwood tree and settled down to watch. Tabby gave her a few anxious moments when she got up and stalked toward the Wagoneer looking as if she meant business, but she was interested only in what was still left of the wildebeest, about five paces from where Lan had parked. She took a leg in her jaws, dragged the kill a short distance away and fed briefly.

Temba, Tombi and Vela sat watching with ears cocked. Tabby called to them and they came forward and fed, sucking and chewing bits of the meat.

The other lioness, Dimples, was lying in the grass nearby. Tabby went off and lay on her belly near Dimples. She tried to rest but the cubs had other ideas. They played all over her. The game they liked best involved discovering which one could walk furthest along her back without falling off. Tabby was extremely patient and – this was interesting – there was never the slightest suggestion that she preferred the normal tawny cub to the two white ones.

After a while the lionesses began to doze off. But suddenly they both sprang up, their eyes fixed intently on the bush at their right. Lan saw the heads of two giraffes peering down over the trees at the young lions. They were clearly intrigued at the sight of the white cubs, which stood out sharply against the surrounding foliage. One of them – rather sensibly, Lan thought – soon moved away to a safer distance. The other one seemed quite incapable of abandoning this uncanny sight.

The lionesses soon lost interest in the giraffes and flopped down to doze again. Eventually the giraffes wandered off.

More than half an hour after the giraffes had gone, a vulture swooped down, aiming to perch in a dead tree near the kill. Lan was startled at the speed of Tabby's reaction. In a second she was on her feet, a tawny surge of angry power, jumping and growling at the circling vulture. The bird of prey saw that Tabby meant business and lolloped off.

This was a Cape vulture, one of the three species of vulture most often seen circling the bushveld skies. Two of them, the lappet-faced vulture and the white-backed vulture, have nested in tall trees in the heart of the Machaton lion range for decades. These settlements imply that lions and other predators have regularly hunted along this reach of the river for even longer, and that the vultures have come to rely on them.

Vultures are probably the only complete scavengers among the bigger birds and animals. They'll eat anything – even lion droppings. In some areas, however, there are fears for the survival of the Cape vulture. In the past, the vulture parents took back chips of bone to their chicks. Now, in those areas the hyenas that once crushed the bones of a kill into small fragments have disappeared. In turn, there are no more bone fragments, because no other predator – not even a lion – can crush bones like a hyena. And as a result, vulture chicks are dying from a calcium deficiency. Some are so weak that they fall to the ground when they try their first flight. Bits of stone and even white china have been found in their nests, an indication that they're searching – desperately and in vain – for new sources of calcium.

But that isn't happening in Timbavati. Spotted hyenas are still here in great numbers, even if, being strictly nocturnal, they're not often seen.

Lan and James went back home without catching another glimpse of the world's only white lions. The days that followed the discovery of the cubs stretched into a week, and then another week, and nobody saw them again. Like a vision, they had vanished. We began to doubt that we had seen them at all.

But the photographs were there; not professional photographs by any means, but they established beyond all doubt that Tabby's litter had included two snow-white cubs.

In the meantime, I continued to track and observe the rest of the pride, which had now become a separate group distinct from Tabby and her cubs and Dimples.

When a lioness in a pride has a litter, she normally withdraws, usually with one or more of the other lionesses, and forms a subgroup for the protection of the cubs. One reason for this is that on a kill, lions can be very vicious and a cub that attempts to defy the strict feeding order is in grave danger of being wounded by a more senior member of the pride. Another reason is that small subgroups can live off smaller animals, such as impala or wildebeest; a full pride or a large subgroup would need to kill a giraffe.

About a week after we lost sight of Tabby and the cubs, I spent most of one afternoon watching nine of the Machaton lions slumbering on open sand in a typical resting place. Shortly before sunset they began to yawn, stretch, walk a few paces . . . and then flop down again. Some lazily groomed themselves. The younger lions stalked one another and played at wrestling.

It was like watching an orchestra warming up, except that it was far more prolonged. The leading lioness of the group, Golden, began to roar softly and repeatedly. Then she stalked off to start a hunt. One by one the others followed. Last to get up, and most reluctant, were Achilles and Agamemnon.

I often saw Golden get the pride moving like this. The only members of the pride to whom she ever gave way, for example on a kill, were the two big males. All the other lions adopted submissive postures or made gestures of appeasement.

Golden, like Achilles and Agamemnon, was, in general, very much concerned with defending the pride's range. Only twice in all the time I've spent watching the pride have I been threatened by a lioness – a mock charge accompanied by a deep rumbling and a thunderclap growl. And both times it was by Golden.

But no matter how much I was caught up in observing the rest of the pride, I could not get the thought of the white cubs out of my mind. By an incredible stroke of luck, the white cubs had been born into the Machaton pride. Although more than two weeks had gone by, I felt confident that I would soon catch up with Temba and Tombi again. Still, whenever I met one of the warden's rangers I couldn't resist inquiring about *amahlope*, the white ones. But the reply from these students of the bush was always the same: "*Asimbonanga*." "We haven't seen them."

October 19 was a scorcher – and dry, dry dry. I'd invited a local farmer friend, Hugh Chittenden, to help me look for the lions. And hopefully to locate the cubs that so many people in the area were now beginning to suspect were a hoax.

We set off in the jeep about eleven A.M. with a rifle, a camera, a sharp knife, a gallon of drinking water and plenty of fruit. The old jeep, dented but undaunted by twenty years of combat with bumpy tracks and bush, riverbeds and rocks, ranged the lions' territory for a good three hours in that brutal heat. Only a few mouthfuls of water and an orange or two remained.

Two o'clock in the afternoon and six miles from Vlak . . . and success at last. There they were, the white cubs, taking their siesta under a spreading shingayi.

As I watched them, I was dimly aware of the shuffling and scuffling as Hugh jostled his camera into position. Click . . . click . . . click. He was working very fast and breathing heavily. This was something far too good to risk missing. Click . . . click . . . click again, as he shifted position and altered focus. Click . . . click . . . click. In no time at all he had run through a whole roll of color film.

The lions were clearly feeling the heat. Tabby was panting at a rate of about 120 gulps of air a minute and the breathing rate of the cubs was not much slower.

They stirred after a while, and we watched with almost reverent awe as this perfectly ordinary lioness walked nonchalantly out of the shade and straight past the jeep, trailed by two little white cubs and their tawny brother.

They went down the dry riverbed and disappeared into the thick bush that skirts the Machaton.

We were sorry to see them go, but we were relieved to know that they were still alive and well – and less vulnerable with every week that passed.

CHAPTER FOUR

Charlotte...and California

MY FATHER BOUGHT THE FARM at Timbavati when I was about five, and I've been intrigued by the bush ever since my first visit. Lan, my younger brother Ian and I spent long periods of our youth at Vlak. We made friends with the local African children and went out with airguns, shooting hare, francolin (a small bird rather like a pheasant) and other game.

In those days everyone did a certain amount of shooting. There's far less now and almost none purely for its own sake. Curiously enough, many people like myself who later became deeply involved in ecology and wildlife management had their first taste of the lure of the bush while out hunting.

Shooting is no longer a sport to me; it is simply a chore. I think most of the people in Timbavati have come around to this view. They all have guns; they need them, both for their own protection and to provide rations, but very few shoot wild animals for sport any more.

Outside the reserves – and Timbavati is only one of about thirty such private reserves in South Africa – the attitudes toward shooting are quite different. The farmers shoot lions and other predators regularly, not for sport, but to deter them from attacking their cattle. I know one farmer in the area who openly boasts that he stopped counting after he had killed two hundred lions. There are also the trophy hunters, who shoot lions for their skins.

I have always wanted to live in the wild, but when I was growing up the only way of doing this would have been to become a game warden. I didn't want to do this, because it involved too many chores like mending fences and offered too few opportunities for close contact with wild animals. There were no courses in wildlife management or ecology at any of the local universities; such courses were hardly available anywhere then, outside of America.

So giving up the idea for the time, I went to Michaelhouse, which was roughly equivalent to an English public school, then went on to Witwatersrand University, where I studied English literature and Zulu. While I was at school and later at university, I used to spend as much time as possible in Timbavati walking in the bush with my father and Jack Mathebula, the tracker.

When I left university, I taught for a while in an African school; I took the job primarily to earn enough money to enable me to spend six or eight months wandering around the wildest part of Africa I could find. To experience virgin Africa for myself, before it was too late, had always been my overriding passion – ever since I was a child at Vlak.

As soon as I saved up what seemed like enough money

for the trip, I set off for the wildest place I knew of, the Okovongo Swamps in northern Botswana. I found an African guide called Masaki and traveled with him in his *mokorro*, a dug-out canoe constructed in a way that hasn't changed significantly since the Stone Age; they are hacked out of a single log and are still widely used in various parts of Africa.

For nearly eight months I lived with Masaki and his family. In all that time I never saw another white man nor spoke a word of English.

It was very wild country, crawling with wildlife – more even than in Timbavati. I carried a shotgun and shot francolin and guinea fowl on the fringe of the swamps. Apart from the gun, all I took with me was a sack of cornmeal – or "mealie meal," as it's called locally – and a camera. The Africans with whom I was traveling knew exactly which plants we could eat: the hearts of palm trees, various nuts, and roots like water lily roots. It was surprisingly good, sustaining food and I remained completely healthy and happy throughout the entire period.

We used to walk or canoe from daybreak until about eleven, then rest up for a few hours in the worst of the heat. In the early afternoon we'd catch a fish or two or shoot something for a meal, and leave again about three.

There were lions there but I didn't see much of them. The people of the bush have developed a habit of avoiding anything that is dangerous. They knew where the lions were, and the lions knew where they were, and by common consent they avoided each other scrupulously.

When I left the Okovongo Swamps, I went back to tracking

lions in Timbavati with Jack for a bit. It was our great hobby – tracking lions – and with Jack there to help me, I seldom lost the spoor. I had done a bit of tracking in Botswana with the bushmen there who are said to be the world's best, but Jack is superior. His remarkable ability could be due partly to the fact that in his youth he had been a highly successful poacher.

Eventually, I ran out of money and had to go back to work. I got an appointment at the same African school and remained there from 1966 until 1971, when I left for America to study wildlife management.

In the meantime, I met Charlotte.

Her parents, the Masons, were English. Her father had worked for many years with the British Colonial Service in India, in Malaya and in the Luangwa Valley, in what used to be Northern Rhodesia. He was every bit as interested in the wild as my father, so immediately Charlotte and I had that in common.

When I met her she was working in television, doing a bit of modeling, voice-overs, graphic design and work in a film library. We were married in her parents' house and spent our honeymoon up the Zambesi, sleeping on the ground, with elephants all round us.

Charlotte is probably the best partner in the world for me – or the worst, according to the way you look at it. She shares my passion for the bush and for living rough among wild animals. Neither of us cares very much about the things that most other people regard as essential – security, a comfortable home, television, stereo, even electricity, if it comes to that: we both prefer candlelight.

She was quite accustomed to mixing with wild animals long before she met me, and remembers going into the bush as a very small child. Her father had always been very careful to bring her up with a healthy respect for animals. If you are careful, he used to tell her, there is no need to be afraid.

Nevertheless, as careful as she was, she had some terrifying experiences.

On one occasion her father was shooting buffalo and he took the whole family along for a picnic – Charlotte, her mother and her younger sister, Chloe. Charlotte was about six at the time.

Mr. Mason went off with his gun and Charlotte's mother started to spread out a picnic lunch on the grass near an anthill. Anthills in this part of Africa, incidentally, are often quite spectacular. Many of them are at least ten feet high, with a base as thick as an old oak tree. They are built out of the red earth of the area and look like medieval fortresses. Also, they're frequently used for shelter by varieties of wildlife a good deal bigger than ants.

The family had brought the dog along with them, a huge Labrador, and while they were preparing for the picnic, he kept sniffing around the anthill. Eventually he plucked up enough courage to go into a hole in the base of it and investigate.

A second later he came flying out again, followed by a large male lion that had been resting inside. At the unexpected sight of the humans, the lion ran off . . . but right in the direction of the buffaloes that Charlotte's father was hunting. Disturbed by the sudden appearance of a lion in their midst, the herd immediately stampeded – straight for the spot that Mrs. Mason had selected for the picnic.

Used to this kind of emergency, Charlotte's mother quickly put the two girls up a tree and climbed into another herself. A few seconds later the herd came thundering through. They had barely missed being trampled to death.

Another time Charlotte was walking in the bush with her father, tracking a leopard that had been mauling the cattle in the area. They had a tracker with them and were wading through some tall grass when for some reason they turned round and saw a couple of fully grown male lions following them. By rights, the lions should have run away as soon as they became aware that there were humans in the vicinity, but these didn't. They just sat down and watched.

"We'd better sit down, too. Very quietly – and wait," Charlotte's father whispered. It must have taken a bit of doing, to sit there silently in the long grass with two lions only a few hundred yards away, but that's exactly what they did. After lying there, watching Charlotte and her father and the tracker for a few minutes, the lions quietly got up and wandered off into the bush.

As a child, Charlotte would sometimes spend the whole night in a tree with her father, when he was trying to shoot leopards. One night he had a young goat on a rope as bait. The two of them sat in the tree for hours watching the bait, Charlotte recalls, when all of a sudden it disappeared. Neither of them had heard anything, nor caught even a glimpse of the leopard. That's how fast a leopard is: the goat just wasn't there anymore.

She was also charged by elephants when she was a child, more times than she can remember. In fact, her father developed a technique for avoiding charging elephants. If the animals were coming straight at the front of the jeep, he would continue to drive right at them until the last moment, then suddenly veer off and do a zig-zag course over that terrible terrain of rocks and gulleys and stumps of trees until he could find a space to backtrack and shake them off.

Charlotte didn't have what might be described as a gentle upbringing by any means.

After we were married I went back to teaching for a while. Then, a few days after Tabs was born, taking advantage of a six-month sabbatical to which I was entitled after three years of teaching, we packed her in a knapsack and set off for Cape Town where we spent the time fishing and sleeping on the beach. The knapsack, incidentally, was not one of those sophisticated devices in which it has now become fashionable to transport small children, but an ordinary shabby canvas one. Tabs grew up in that knapsack. She was hardly ever out of it until she was two years old.

As soon as we returned from Cape Town, I received word that I had been accepted into a course in wildlife management at Humboldt State University in Arcata, California. Several months previously I had written to Archie Mossman, a wildlife management professor at Humboldt who had spent six years in Rhodesia researching game ranching on exactly the same sort of terrain as the Lowveld. I explained to him that I wanted to enroll in his department because I had always wanted to study ecology and wildlife management on a proper scientific basis.

Acceptance letter in hand, I took my savings, such as they were, and set off for California in late 1971. Charlotte and Tabs followed me out a few weeks later, when I had established myself in a trailer caravan which Archie Mossman allowed me to park on his land – he had twelve acres of redwood country not far from the university. That was our home for the next three years.

By conventional standards, of course, it wasn't much of a

home. The trailer had a small gas stove in one corner, but it only warmed that one corner, and it can be very cold in redwood country.

Charlotte found a marvelous neighbor who ran a nursery and looked after Tabs during the day for us. This enabled Charlotte to go out and work, to help support us. She sliced salmon on the wharf, she made pizzas in a pizza parlor, she served beer in a bar, she even sold insurance door to door. Eventually she got a very good job as administrative assistant to local dentists Gary Tucker and Joe Zamboni – the same Joe Zamboni who later visited us in Timbavati and photographed the mating of Agamemnon and Tabby.

In the meantime, I was working day and night at my studies and managed to fulfill all the course requirements in a little under three years.

But it wasn't all work. Fishing is the second great passion of my life, and our trailer was parked beside a salmon river. We would often go fishing for salmon and steelhead (sea trout). Tabs came everywhere with us. We'd just throw her into the knapsack and cart her around wherever we went. Even at that age, she knew it all; she knew exactly where the best fish were to be found, far better than I did. And living in the trailer out in the redwoods, she became completely accustomed to the outdoor life from the time she could walk. We often used to stay out all night and sleep on the beaches. Tabs adored sleeping out. In fact, she still does. She's always pestering me to bring her out to sleep in the open, with the lions.

When I had finished my course work, toward the end of 1974, I still had to do a thesis requiring at least six months' fieldwork. That's what brought me back to Timbavati and the Machaton pride. For the last four months, from the moment I decided to narrow the scope of my thesis and go back to Timbavati to study one particular pride of lions, we couldn't do anything except think about getting back to Africa. We talked Africa, we dreamed about Africa, we even held African parties.

Charlotte was every bit as eager to get back to the bush as I was, even keener maybe. She once said to me that she has tried to analyze what it is about Africa that holds such an appeal for her, but she just can't pin it down — and neither can I.

It's something in your blood. A combination of the climate, the landscape, the wildlife, the whole atmosphere. You somehow feel that you're missing everything when you're not there.

Chapter Five

Return to Timbavati

When we arrived back in africa in early 1975, my father offered me his camp at Vlak for a year as a base from which to do my research. My sole equipment for the fieldwork was a notebook, a borrowed rifle and camera, and a jeep.

It was during the next few months that I spent so many hours trekking the area, mainly with Jack Mathebula. We got to know the terrain and the lions' routes, catching glimpses of the Machaton lions and of others, singly and in groups. Soon we came to know them well enough to distinguish one pride from another.

We were very lucky in coming across the Machaton lions because, as it turned out, they are one of the few prides in the Timbavati area that might be described as a resident pride. About nine-tenths of their range lies entirely within Timbavati, with the rest extending into the Kruger National Park. Most of the prides in the area have half their ranges inside the Kruger Park and the other half in Timbavati. It would have been difficult to cover their territories as freely as I wanted to and as thoroughly as I was able to do in the case of the Machaton range.

Concentrating on the area in the immediate vicinity of the camp, Jack and I would drive out into the bush until we found spoor, then get out and track them on foot until we came across them, usually asleep under a shingayi. Then we would creep away and return later in the jeep to study them at length and in detail, until finally we were able to identify each of the Machaton lions at a glance.

There were two other prides in the area whose ranges fringed on the Machaton range. One of these we called the Velvet Paws pride, because of their velvety paws. The other we named the Flop Ear pride, because one of the young male lions has a very floppy ear. There are also a couple of unnamed prides to the south, but I never had a chance to observe them in any detail.

About the time that the white lions were born, the Flop Ear pride consisted of fifteen lions and the Velvet Paws pride had nine. The total number of lions in any pride, however, is subject to constant fluctuations. This is largely due to the frequency with which the lionesses bear cubs and the fact that the mortality rate among these cubs is very high. Also contributing to the fluctuation is the fact that the young males are almost invariably thrown out by the pride when they reach the age of two and a half or three.

We soon discovered that the character of the prides varied a great deal. The Flop Ear pride, also known as the Sohebele lions because their range centers on the Sohebele game-viewing lodge, are much more aggressive than the Machaton lions.

Charlotte had several unpleasant experiences with the Flop Ear pride. On one occasion, when she was helping me by making observations of the other prides in the area, she was in the closed Wagoneer with Tabs and some of her friends and drove right into the middle of the Flop Ear pride who turned out to be, as she put it at the time, "quite interestingly aggressive." The lions would hide behind the trees and then charge right up to the car, which was pretty frightening to everyone inside – even if they were behind glass. Whenever that happened, Charlotte would reverse a bit into the bush and wait for a few minutes before following them again. In all, they charged the Wagoneer about six times that morning. One male even jumped up and put his paws on the side of the Wagoneer. Charlotte believes that they were only "playfully aggressive," but the risk she took that day was immense. A lion could easily smash the windows of a car with one blow of its paw – and he wouldn't feel a thing.

There were other differences between the prides. The Flop Ear pride seems to rest mainly on the sand of dried-up riverbeds. I've seen my pride in a riverbed only once in nearly two years. Eating preferences also differ, not only from pride to pride but from area to area. My pride and most of the prides in Timbavati seem to avoid buffalo. Yet in one area of East Africa, where George Schaller did his research, buffalo comprised more than half of the kills.

Lion prides are almost as individualistic in their habits and preferences as human families – as are all animals that live in such social units. That's one reason why I believe there is a need for much more research into the behavior and environmental needs of all animals before plans for wildlife management can be properly set into motion.

Just as difficult as discovering the composition of my own pride, and learning something about the immediately adjoining ones, was the problem of establishing the nature of their environment, the routes they used and the purposes to which they put the widely differing amenities of their range. To do this, I worked from aerial photographs, ordnance survey maps and maps which I drew for myself featuring details of importance to the lions which did not appear on official maps.

If you look at the map on p. 76, you can see that between five and six miles of the Machaton are almost completely encircled by black soil plains. In the rainy season, these plains support a rich kind of grass that is highly favored by grazing animals such as wildebeest – it's actually prime wildebeest country. When the rains come, the grazing animals tend to congregate on these black soil plains and the lions do their hunting there and return to the Machaton to rest.

In the dry season, the game is normally found along the Machaton because that's where the only water is, apart from the other dam, the marsh and the perennial spring. In particular, the browsers – animals like giraffe and kudu that almost exclusively eat the leaves of trees instead of grass – tend to congregate along the Machaton because the trees along the edge of the river have access to underground water. Even when the riverbed dries out completely to ankle-deep golden sand, there is water deep under this sand, and the roots of the trees can penetrate through to the water so that the trees always have green leaves. These attract the browsers, which in turn ensures that the lions have a year-round supply of prey.

If you were to take a cross section anywhere along the Machaton, quite close to the river, you would first have a fringe of thick riverine bush, trees up to twenty or thirty feet

75

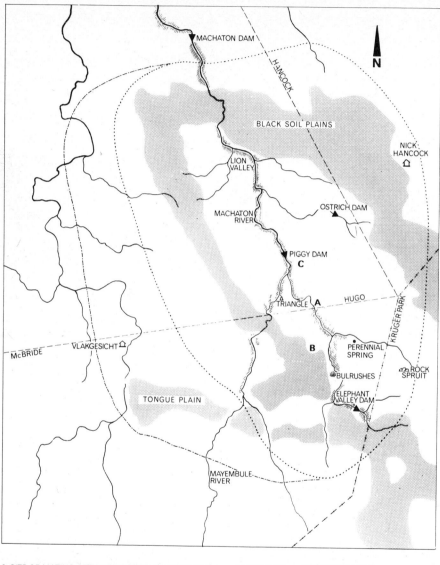

A SITE OF MATING BETWEEN TABBY & AGAMEMNON
B FIRST SIGHTING OF WHITE CUBS
C FIRST SIGHTING OF PHUMA—THE NEW WHITE CUB

– – – – – – TRACK/BOUNDARY
+ + + + + + FENCE
· · · · · · · · · DRY SEASON RANGE
· – · · – · · – EXTENDED RAINY SEASON RANGE
ALKALINE PLAINS

one mile

The Range of the Machaton Lions

76

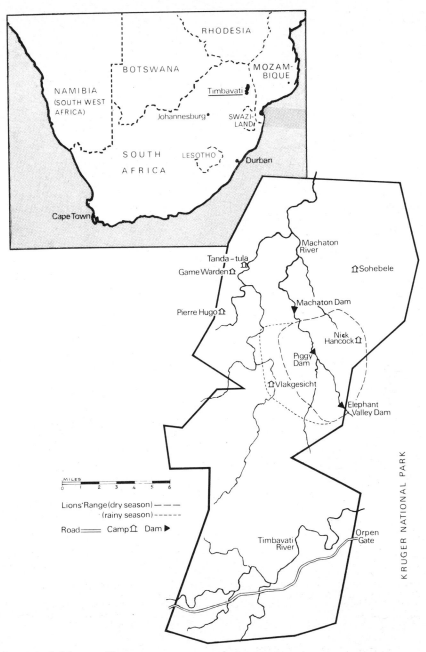

RHODESIA

BOTSWANA

MOZAM-
BIQUE

NAMIBIA
(SOUTH WEST
AFRICA)

Timbavati

Johannesburg

SWAZI-
LAND

SOUTH
AFRICA

LESOTHO

Durban

Cape Town

Machaton
River

Tanda-tula

Game Warden

Sohebele

Pierre Hugo

Machaton Dam

Nick
Hancock

Piggy
Dam

Vlakgesicht

Elephant
Valley Dam

MILES
0 1 2 3 4 5 6

Lions' Range (dry season) — — —
(rainy season) - - - - -

Road === Camp ⌂ Dam ▶

Timbavati
River

Orpen
Gate

KRUGER NATIONAL PARK

Timbavati Nature Reserve

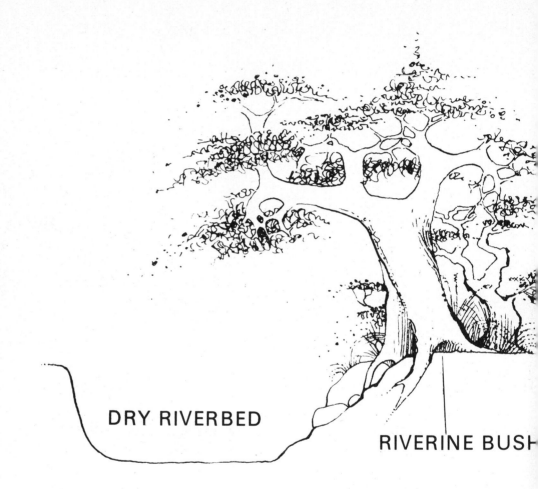

The Machaton River and the Surrounding Terrain—A Cross Section

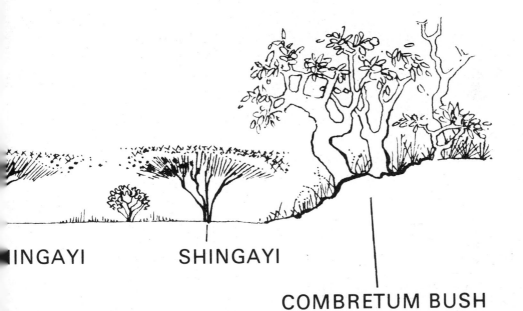

HINGAYI   SHINGAYI

COMBRETUM BUSH

ALKALINE PLAIN

high, nourished by the underground water. This is where the lions shelter in windy, unpleasant weather and where they conceal their newborn cubs.

The alkaline plain between the riverine bush and the dark soil plain is flat, level land with stunted trees, no grass, nothing prickly and unpleasant, and no ticks because of the lack of grass. This is where the lions like to rest, ideally under the shade of a shingayi tree.

The shingayi is seldom taller than ten feet and provides a wide, umbrella-like canopy. Because it is extremely broad in relation to its height, its shape provides the maximum of shade. Also because the tree is low, the area of shade does not vary much during the course of a day, as would be the case with a taller tree. Thus, a lion lying under a shingayi doesn't have to move about nearly so often to stay within the shaded area. And since lions are almost fanatical in their determination to conserve energy that suits them fine.

There is even another factor which enters into their choice of the shingayi. For some reason, both wildebeest and warthog have over the centuries developed a habit of rolling around on their backs under shingayi trees. In doing so, they remove the last vestiges of grass roots and any other unpleasant prickly things that might disturb the lions' rest.

The lions hunt in the surrounding bush, largely along the ecotone, the fringe area where the plain merges into the bush. They do this because there's enough cover there to enable them to stalk their prey unseen, and yet it's not thick enough to impede their movements when they are hunting as a pride.

By following the lions on foot, I soon discovered that my pride had a number of routes linking the various parts of the range which they used time and time again. Most of these

I worked from ordnance survey maps and aerial photographs to establish the routes the lions used and the exact nature of their environment.

TOP: For protein we literally lived off the bush – mainly on impala shot by me and butchered and cooked by Charlotte.

BOTTOM: One of Tabitha's pets was a baby warthog known as PP (Pathetic Pig).

RIGHT: The other great passion of my life, apart from watching lions, has always been fishing: here I'm fishing for trout in Lesotho.

FOLLOWING PAGES: Some of our neighbors at Timbavati . . .

The variety of wildlife here is unparalleled. We're surrounded by species which vary from large animals like giraffe and elephant right down to the tiniest varieties of mosquito and fireflies. PREVIOUS PAGE (clockwise): giraffe, elephant, cheetah, impala. THIS PAGE (clockwise): vulture, steinbok, jackal, impala again – by far the most numerous of our Timbavati neighbors.

There are 1,400 zebras in Timbavati, but it's very hard to photograph them except like this, from the rear. Among the most timid members of the reserve's wildlife family, they always scatter at the first appearance of our jeep.

In all the time we spent watching our pride, we seldom saw the adult males indulge in any sort of play with the cubs. Agamemnon largely ignored his trio and left Tabby to care for them.

ABOVE: Of the two pride males, Achilles is more alert, more of a leader. It seems to me that Achilles and Agamemnon are brothers, probably twins, and it's likely that they've spent part of their lives as nomads, hunting together, which would account for the close bond between them.

RIGHT: Tabby is one of the most casual of mothers. Right from the beginning she showed no fear either of us or the jeep, often leading the cubs right out to where we were parked.

Sometimes it wasn't easy to pick out all the members of the group because the shade helped them to blend into the landscape. But the white cubs were always easy to spot. And once we'd found them, we could go back to the camp to eat and rest, knowing that they'd stay put all day.

ABOVE: We realized that if they were to survive it was possible that at some stage they might need help from us. In many ways the arrival of the white cubs caused us a few headaches – yet we all found them utterly irresistible.

OVERLEAF: Achilles and Agamemnon are almost always together. They frequently sit back to back, like a pair of bookends, almost as if posing for a calendar picture.

routes lay along the alkaline plains, where there were well-established game paths frequently used and kept well open by buffalo and rhino. As a general rule, the lions would choose the easiest path, particularly if the path avoided the long grass and was relatively free both of ticks and thorns.

Before I became thoroughly acquainted with the lions' routes, I often traveled, with the aid of a compass, by a more direct route from one point to the next. I soon discovered that the extra energy needed to wade through the long grass and thick bush far exceeded the effort needed to negotiate the lions' slightly longer route. In terms of time and effort, the lions' bush roads could not have been better mapped out. One of their rather circuitous trails between two dams might be about two miles long, compared with a straight-line distance of just over a mile. Yet walking the lions' path I might do the journey fifteen minutes faster – and with much less pain and exertion – than by ploughing through the tangle of scrub and trees along the direct route.

So by walking the area, with map and compass, I was able to draw up my own maps, marking out the lions' routes and giving names to the various places where we most often sighted them: the Plains, Lion Valley, the Bulrushes, Piggy Dam, Elephant Dam and the Triangle, a triangular area where two spruits, or small dried-up riverbeds, joined the main river.

Soon I had a fairly good idea where the lions were likely to be found at any hour of the day or night.

We also used to track the lions by listening to them roaring at night and marking in the sand outside the rondavel the direction from which the roars appeared to come. The

Machaton lions rarely, if ever, roar during the day, but at night we could hear them quite clearly from the camp. Charlotte was particularly adept at identifying our lions and conditioned herself to wake up every night at about three o'clock to go outside and listen. As soon as the lions started to roar, she would mark the direction by pointing, with her arm extended, toward the place where the roars were coming from. She would then bring her arm down and draw a line toward her body in the sand. We found this method far more accurate than marking the sand by foot, which was sometimes as much as ten degrees off. In the morning I would take a compass and, with a tracker, I would walk along the bearing indicated by Charlotte until we came across either the lions or their spoor.

Before long we were able to dispense with the compass, because we could tell from a glance at Charlotte's mark in the sand where they were most likely to be and head straight there. Lions are terrible creatures of habit; we kept finding them in the same handful of resting places. After the first few weeks, I could usually find them by simply taking out the jeep and visiting all their resting places in turn.

Charlotte sometimes came out tracking the lions with me, bringing Tabs with her, naturally, but the rest of the time she was busy getting the camp organized, setting up a play school for Tabs and a few of her African friends, and establishing a routine which included some basic butchery. For protein we literally lived off the bush – almost entirely on impala shot by me and butchered and turned into delicious steaks and stews and roasts and sausages and meatballs by Charlotte. We even had impala kebabs and spaghetti Bolognese based on minced impala.

It sounds monotonous, but it wasn't. Sometimes she

would wrap the impala flesh in pawpaw skins and leave it for a few days; this tenderizes it and gives it a most delicious flavor. Or, when she made kebabs, she would marinate the meat in soy sauce for a few days and use a lot of rosemary and it tasted just like lamb. When she made stew, she put in less rosemary and it tasted like steak.

Biltong was another of our bush specialties, often prepared jointly by Charlotte and myself because of all the work involved. We make it in the cool of winter, mainly from impala, though you can make it from almost any game, including giraffe and even ostrich. First we cut the meat into tongue-shaped strips from the legs, saddle and rump of the animal. Hence the name *biltong*: from the Africaans *bil* meaning rump, and *tong* meaning tongue. The next step is to sprinkle the strips with a little vinegar, salt and pepper, and spices like ground coriander seeds. The following day we hang the meat on wires in the shade, under a tree or in an open shed, so that the cool breezes can get to it. In this way the meat becomes completely dry within three weeks – and quite safe to eat for up to a year. We would often take biltong with us on long treks through the bush. Pure protein, it's an extremely sustaining and nourishing snack. The Cape bushmen protected themselves from bad times by drying antelope meat in this way long before the first European settlers arrived in southern Africa.

We ate extremely well at Vlak. In fact, on the rare occasions when we visited friends living in so-called civilized circumstances, we found their veal and chicken comparatively tasteless.

But there were problems. The baboons were a nuisance at first, though again Charlotte found the solution. Quite often, when we were away from the camp, the baboons would break in and attack our food supplies. Once, just after Charlotte had gone to Acornhoek to stock up, they broke in and ripped the mesh out of a food bin, took an entire month's supply of fruit and vegetables and squashed them up against the walls, then tore up all our paintings and maps and books. The mess was unbelievable. I tried shooting a couple of them after that but it never did any good; they kept coming back.

Then Charlotte suddenly remembered an old colonial remedy – the Tabasco Sauce and Orange Trick. It worked like a charm. She got a whole sack of oranges, scooped out a hole in the top of each one and poured in a little Tabasco. Then she placed them all around the camp and we went out to watch the lions. When we got back the oranges were gone, but so were the baboons – permanently. They never came near the place again.

When you study animals, the first thing you have to do is forget about human priorities and go onto the schedule of the animals you are studying. So we adopted the lions' routine; the lions dictated our whole way of life. Sometimes we would sleep out all night, on mattresses spread out on the floor of the jeep, feeling secure inside our cage though a bit cramped.

When the moon was bright, we would drive around all night, following the lions so that I could learn their routes and take notes on the frequency with which they used them. Then, like the lions, we would often go back home and sleep through the heat of the day, waking up in the evening around the time the lions would start to move about again.

The best part of a summer day in the bushveld is the still, quiet pre-dawn time, when the sky is just beginning to pale and veils of mist lie over the dew-laden grasses and under the trees, and the birds open up with their pre-dawn chorus. We'd often get up at first light, half past four or five, and after a cup of hot *rooibos*, that's tea, we'd take the compass bearing Charlotte had made in the sand an hour or two earlier and set off, Charlotte, Tabs, Jack and myself, taking along camera and compass and a supply of oranges, biltong, books and tea, plus my pipe and plenty of tobacco.

As we drove out of camp, we might disturb a herd of kudu bulls browsing by the side of the track. These powerful antelope can jump tremendous heights. They are wary and alert, with large, sensitive ears. Sometimes if they were not too frightened by the jeep, they would stop again a short distance from the track, watching us with anxious eyes and flicking tails.

On we'd go then, and the only sound we could hear above the rumble and rattle of the jeep was the shrieking of the francolin as they darted ahead of us on blurred feet, frantically racing from under the front wheels. Their plumage was almost perfect camouflage against the brown earth and bleached grass, except for their conspicuous scarlet heads.

I've always admired the way a mother francolin protects her young. Sensing danger, she will fly away from their position with a fusillade of clucks and squawks, feigning injury by dragging a wing. It's a superb performance staged in the hope of luring the pursuer further and further away from her brood.

Then we might see a couple of old giraffe bulls, dark with age, surveying us curiously over the treetops before loping off to a safe distance, or a herd of wildebeest resting in a safe patch of open sand, or sometimes a lone tortoise ambling along in the middle of the track.

Suddenly we might spot some fresh lion tracks going

through a dry riverbed. We'd stop immediately and Jack and I would jump out to have a closer look. How many lions? Two, maybe three. We might follow the lions' road for a bit on foot, past an old, bare marula tree, past stumps of dead leadwood, then on through another dried-up riverbed. Suddenly, no more tracks. This meant that they had branched off somewhere, and so we would have to go back a bit and look for the one fragment of spoor that would tell us which direction they had gone off in. After a time either Jack or I would find it, and by then I'd know exactly which route they were branching off to join. We could take a shortcut there in the jeep, and Jack and I would get out and try to pick up the spoor again. If we were lucky, we'd find the spot where the lions had crossed the route and perhaps also discover that the original three we'd been tracking had now been joined by six or seven other members of the pride.

Back to the jeep and off we'd go again, heading toward the nearest of their favorite resting places, around a bumpy, grassy corner, and suddenly there they'd be – our pride, as likely as not stretched out under a shingayi. Achilles and Agamemnon might give us a casual glance before dismissing us as totally uninteresting and subsiding with an exhausted sigh on the sand. I would be busy the whole time making notes of all sorts, right down to their panting rate. Sometimes it was difficult to pick out all the members of the group as the shade helped them to blend into the landscape. It's very easy to mistake lions for boulders; it's even possible to miss a large lioness lying down in six inches of grass a short distance away.

After watching the males for a while, we might edge forward slowly, passing them without eliciting from them the slightest sign that they recognized us. Then we'd creep

102

toward the fringe of trees on the edge of a sandy patch, where the remainder of the subgroup was resting. Suddenly one of the young teenage males, the ones we called the Three Musketeers, might get to his feet and walk toward the jeep with a purposeful look. When that happened, I'd stop the jeep again, and we'd all wait, absolutely silent, as the Musketeer came closer and closer, swinging his tail and staring straight at us. Another of the Musketeers might grunt and get up to follow him, and we'd have two of them sniffing around the jeep. These young lions were very inquisitive and seemed neither shy nor hostile, but it was still reassuring to have the cage around us.

After several hours of detailed observation, during which I'd photograph them again and again and make notes of all their actions and interactions, we'd go back to the camp to eat and rest, knowing that they would stay put until sunset, when we could go straight to the same spot, find them again and take it from there.

From the moment we discovered the white lions everything changed – and yet nothing changed. We still went on watching lions every day. I had to, for the sake of my thesis.

Strange as it may seem, the fact that Temba and Tombi were white was actually quite extraneous to my thesis. Their unprecedented coloring could even have proved an obstacle to me, as the Machaton pride might no longer be considered typical. I decided to take it in my stride, however, and simply record what happened. But it was impossible to remain academically detached. I felt from the outset a growing sense of responsibility toward them.

If they were going to survive, it was probable that at

103

some stage they would need human assistance. If so, what would be the best way of helping them? If one of them happened to be injured, say at a kill, would the wisest thing be to dart it with a tranquilizing drug and bring it up in captivity, in a fenced-off area or even a zoo?

And what if I lost track of the young white cubs for a week or two? It had happened once, immediately after we had discovered them, and it could happen again. If it did, and one of the cubs happened to be injured while we were out of touch with the pride, it could easily be abandoned by the others and would soon die. Perhaps the best approach would be to dart one of them and fit it with a transmitter collar which would emit a radio signal. With a receiver we could then keep track of the lions by tuning in and discovering exactly where they were at any given moment.

In many ways the arrival of the white cubs complicated our lives and forced us to face up to some of the most profound issues of ecology and wildlife management.

They caused us a lot of headaches. And yet we found them utterly irresistible.

CHAPTER SIX

Pattern for Survival

TWO DAYS AFTER HUGH and I found Tabby and her cubs
again, some members of our pride invaded Jack's camp at
night. He and his family heard nothing, but the next morning
Jack found a chewed hoe handle and a lot of lion tracks, big
and small. One ax was missing altogether.

Following the spoor, he found the ax more than two
hundred yards away.

Later that afternoon Jack and I trailed the lions in the
jeep. As usual, we saw a lot of other wildlife — hundreds of
impala, a big herd of blue wildebeest, zebra, a group of
graceful kudu cows, two jackals, a family of waterbuck, each
with its distinctive white "target ring" on its rump, and a
Bateleur eagle high in a dead tree.

Two giraffes peered soulfully at us, reminding me of
their apt Zulu name, *amadlulamiti* — "those that surpass the
trees."

A bird, a lilac-breasted roller, swooped across our path

to settle with a flutter on a thorn bush. One of nature's most spectacular miniatures, it is called *uvivi* in Zulu. The false dawn gets its local name, *ngovivi*, from the roller's blue and lilac, turquoise and brown.

The lions' tracks were following a familiar route and I marveled again at their efficient use of the terrain. Finally, at about 4.30 P.M. we crossed the Machaton to the Triangle to find Tabby and her cubs of five to six weeks lolling on the white sand. Shortly before sundown Temba, Tombi and Vela came to life.

To any animal that may have been watching the scene from the leadwood tree under which we had parked, it must have seemed quite an incongruous scene: two humans in a vehicle covered by a cage of iron bars, now and again bursting into surprised laughter; and, beyond, the three furry objects of their mirth — two white and one brown — rolling and tumbling about like kittens.

In the waning light the cubs ran through part of what we were soon to recognize as their regular play repertoire. Stalk a Tail, Run and Swat, Pick-Up Sticks and Pig in the Middle. These were their favorites. Temba, the little white male, was already showing a daredevil streak missing in Tombi and in Vela, his slightly smaller brother.

Temba couldn't resist the twitching tail of an adult lion. We watched him make an elaborate stalk on the black tip of his mother's tail, which moved as she snoozed. He squirmed the last few yards on his stomach. Then, like a domestic cat about to spring, he wiggled his bottom. A leap and he was on his quarry, giving it a sharp nip. As casual and indulgent with her offspring as always, Tabby raised her head a few inches off the sand, gave a mild mewing protest and sank back into slumber.

Run and Swat was a nifty game for two. On our left, Vela in brown. On our right, Temba in white. Between them, three lion-lengths of soft sand. Temba to charge . . . and off he went, bounding and prancing. As he neared Vela, they both reared up on hind legs and cuffed one another.

Tombi, with coy discretion, usually waited for one of her brothers to initiate play. But she was always ready to join them in a tug-of-war over a stick. Or in a bout of Pig in the Middle. This was a game in which the three cubs stood in line, the two on the outside trying to nip the bottom of the pig in the middle. When one succeeded, the pig would swing round and take a swipe at its assailants . . . leaving its flank open to attack from the other side. The trick, it seemed, was to avoid getting caught in the middle.

Since then, of course, we've spent many hours watching the cubs at play, and have been able to analyze and, indeed, even predict their daily play patterns. In all the time we've been observing the pride, I've seldom seen the adult males indulge in any of this sort of play. They usually kept well clear of such sessions, and on the few occasions that Temba, the spunky one, dared to jump on Agamemnon's rump, he was swiftly warned off with an irritable growl. The cubs seldom went near Achilles. It was almost as if Tabby seemed to have some way of warning her cubs not to be too free with the adult males.

The games invariably ended in a good-natured free-for-all. But already, subconsciously, the cubs were rehearsing for their role in adult life. Many of the postures and movements they used when playing were scaled-down versions of some of the behavior patterns of full-grown lions.

The games of young lions can be roughly divided into two categories: a simulation of those actions that lions use when killing prey, such as jumping on the back of the lioness; and a simulation of those actions that lions use on the rare occasions when they have to fight each other, for example, standing up on their hind legs and clawing at one another. The cubs' play serves the double function of preparing them for the hunt and also for preparing them for the techniques they will need for survival as full-grown lions when they will have to defend themselves against nomads or assert themselves within the social ranks of their own pride.

But fascinating and lovable as we found the cubs, we could never overlook the fact that lions are potentially highly dangerous. Many of the wild animals that surrounded us were – the elephants most of all. Even lions are wary when there are elephants around.

As a kind of security measure, all the camps in the reserve have some type of protective stockade around them. There's no way that these stockades could keep out a determined elephant, or a determined anything, for that matter. But like the cage around our jeep, they give you a sense of security.

Timbavati has one resident breeding herd of elephants, the sole breeding herd outside a national park in the country until very recently, and elephants with calves will attack anything. The camp occupants, listening to their trumpeting at night, just have to keep their fingers crossed and hope the herd is not headed in their direction. Some of the camps have flares which can be fired to frighten them off; in others, if they get too close, we just fire a few rifle shots over their heads and hope that will work.

Lions, and more often leopards, frequently get into the enclosures at night. No dog can ever be considered safe from prowling leopards. Apparently they are a very popular delicacy with leopards, and consequently property owners tend to discourage pets on the reserve. Even if the fencing could be made impregnable, dogs still wouldn't be safe. A few years back, a game warden's small dog was attacked from the air in front of his very eyes. An ominous shadow . . . and whoosh, it was gone. Snatched aloft in the talons of an eagle.

No barrier will keep the snakes out either; we always kept a serum kit on hand in the camp and used flashlights at night to make certain that we didn't step on anything likely to strike back.

We seldom saw the lions near Vlak, but every few weeks during the summer, we found lion tracks around our quarters. At night, strangely, lions seemed to lose some of their instinctive fear of human smells. But I think that the main reason for these frequent visits was that our camp lay on a main route leading to one of their principal hunting areas, called Tongue Plain because of its shape.

Bushveld nights are clear and crisp and sound travels far. A jackal howls . . . and on the still air, from across the Plains, comes an answering howl. These are the black-backed jackals, an everyday sight in the reserve. There are a few, very few, side-striped jackals, a rare species down here.

At midnight one night, shortly after the hyena's familiar *whoo-ep, whoo-ep* had floated in from the distant bush, I heard another familiar sound that seemed to come from right outside our rondavel. It was the quiet, communicating *oo* sound of a lion. I crept to the door and edged it open. There they were – at least four lions. But they'd heard the door open and immediately ran away.

Next day we judged from the tracks that no fewer than seven of the Machaton pride had paid us a visit.

Toward the end of the year, the first of the good rains came. Almost overnight little green daggers stabbed up through the damp soil of the Plains. And in a few weeks carpets of new grass had transformed bushveld clearings into verdant playgrounds for Temba, Tombi and Vela.

One afternoon I went out with Victor Hugo, a university student and son of our neighbor at Vlak, Dr. Pierre Hugo. Parked at the edge of a glade we had ringside seats for the cubs' games. We'd found them the way we frequently did these days – by watching the giraffes. Whenever we came across a group of giraffes staring curiously down into the bush, it was a fair bet it was the white cubs they were staring at.

The cubs romped and wrestled, playing the games that would no longer be games when they grew up. At one point Temba leaped up and dropped a little paw on Vela's rump, rolling him over and nipping him in the nape of the neck – in precisely the way his mother would deal with a wildebeest.

A soft rain had begun to fall, and Temba got it into his head that it would be great sport to pin Tombi down in the mud. Then Vela tried to be King of the Castle by climbing right on top of the snarling pair. The dark mud had streaked the white cubs making them look more like zebras than the fearsome beasts they seemed to think they were.

The elders were reveling in the sudden coolness. Achilles lay on his back, his legs spread-eagled, enjoying the rain falling on his belly. When Temba, normally most respectful

110

toward Achilles, summoned up enough courage to give the old man's tail a tug, the big male merely moved off a few paces, without even protesting, out of the play zone.

Agamemnon had been lying a few yards away, his eyes half-closed and rain droplets filtering through his massive beard. Achilles joined him, and I'll always remember the picture those two close companions made, lying back to back, almost like bookends, their heads held regally, half turned away, surveying their world.

Having failed to interest the pride males in their play routines, Temba and Tombi decided to investigate the motionless monster, our jeep. The two cubs came right up to it and we could clearly see that their noses and lips were well pigmented and their eyes only a slightly paler yellow than Vela's. Tabby, as usual, kept a casually watchful eye on them.

Nearby was a tree that had been pushed over by an elephant. It rested against an adjoining upright tree making a ramp that the cubs couldn't resist. Vela was the first to venture up, with Tombi close behind. Last for a change, Temba charged up after them and then all three tumbled to the ground.

They tried it again. It was Vela who finally succeeded. Up he climbed, going higher and higher until he was almost twelve feet up. Somehow he had managed to wedge himself in a fork of the vertical tree. He looked down. This was no place for a young lion. He shuffled uncomfortably. Then he gave a strangled mew, for all the world like a domestic kitten in difficulties of its own making.

Tabby heard him now and walked carefully over to the sloping tree. Seeing her close at hand, Vela seemed to gain confidence. He scrambled free and slithered down the ramp toward her. Then, inevitably, over the side he went. But the six-foot fall to the soft earth didn't seem to bother him at all and he was soon frolicking with his brother and sister again.

Vic and I were fascinated by this performance, but the incident was very disturbing in a way, for it underlined the concern we felt for the young white cubs. As Vic put it in a diary he wrote at the time:

"The green fields in which these innocent tussles took place were the sharpest reminder we'd had yet of the severe handicap facing Temba and Tombi. If they stay as white as they are – and there's still not the slightest hint of any significant darkening of their coats – how can they ever hope to hunt with any degree of success? In the brown of winter or the green of summer? By night or by day?"

At best, we realized that the young white lions would be severely handicapped. Over the millennia, evolution must have produced mutants of this type before, and the fact that none of them appears ever to have survived could very well attest to their inability to fend for themselves.

Some zoologists believe that in the past, when there were lions in many parts of the world where they now no longer exist, there was probably a much greater color variation than is found today. For example, before the Romans wiped out the lions in North Africa by rounding them up to feature as attractions in their arenas there would have probably been a strain of very pale, almost white lions in that area: lions would have needed that coloring as camouflage in the Sahara Desert.

Most animals carry genes that are known as recessive genes – that is, genes capable of throwing up a whole range of variations, including color variations. And where this color variation proves useful in some way to the animal, it can

112

become the dominant strain. The peppered moth is a classic example of such an adaptation. Normally the moth is lichen-colored. It is so camouflaged to protect it from its predators, in this case birds. The lichen coloring makes the moth almost invisible on trees and even brown buildings. This particular moth carried a recessive gene capable of throwing up a black strain. In most places in the world where the lichen coloring was a better camouflage, the black strain remained a rarity. But in the Midlands and the North of England, where the buildings on which the moths spend most of their time are black with soot, black became the dominant strain, and the normal lichen-colored moth far less common.

In the same way, leopards have turned up a black strain and in certain areas this has persisted because in some ways it is an advantage for a leopard to be black, since it hunts at night. On the other hand, it is also an advantage for a leopard to be spotted, because that way it can hide all day in a tree with its kill, unnoticed and therefore undisturbed by other predators or scavengers. This seems to be a case in which evolution has turned up two totally workable solutions; so you find black leopards and spotted leopards existing side by side.

As far as lions are concerned, however, I can see no set of circumstances that would ever make it advantageous for them to be white, so I don't really see this white strain developing unless man steps in and does a certain amount of stage managing.

There was one thing that puzzled me at first. If a strain of white lions does exist in this part of South Africa, why has it never shown up before? If there had been white lions here at some point, you would at least expect to find a white lion skin somewhere.

After further thought, however, I realized that Timbavati is almost completely uninhabited. Even knowing of the existence of the white lions, the owner of one part of their range has seen them only once.

The game warden, however observant he may be, has to patrol over two hundred square miles of wilderness, and the lions are just one of his concerns. The high mortality rate among cubs and the fact that lionesses keep their young well hidden in the riverine bush makes the chances of young white cubs being seen in this area very slight.

It is quite possible that white lions cubs have been born here in the past and simply disappeared before anyone caught a glimpse of them. As it happened, we were unusually lucky to spot them when they were only a few weeks old. We were also particularly lucky to find them again and be in a position to keep in touch with them as they grew up.

As Vic and I watched the cubs that day I was aware that Temba and Vela as young males would face their most critical period between two and three.

Until they are around two years old, they will be almost entirely dependent on Tabby and the other lionesses of the pride, who will do all their hunting for them. Like all male lions, they will then face one of the major challenges inherent in the pride system. As the cubs approach the age of three, Achilles and Agamemnon, if they are still in control, may start regarding them as rivals, particularly sexual rivals. The cubs, whether white or tawny, would stand very little chance against the lions unless one or both of the pride males are considerably slowed down by age. So far they don't seem to be showing any signs of weakening.

Achilles and Agamemnon have probably remained on top for so long simply because, as a team, they could more easily cope with insurrection from within the pride, or invasion by nomads from outside – and they will probably remain on top for a long time to come.

Temba and Vela may have to be driven out; they might decide to leave the pride and become nomads, living either together or separately, looking for their own worlds to conquer. Temba, if he walked out of the pride alone, could well be sentencing himself to death by starvation. His white coat would stand out like a beacon at night and he couldn't possibly hope for the hunting success of an ordinary lion.

There are people who will argue that a fully grown lion is such a formidable beast that he'll be able to kill his prey and survive regardless of his coloring. I don't believe this. In order to make a kill, lions must be very close to their prey – no further than twenty or thirty yards away – because all of their prey are capable of running faster than they can. To catch the fleeing animal before it has had time to reach its maximum running speed, lions need the element of surprise: camouflage. And this the white cubs do not have.

Other hazards await Temba, and Vela too, should they venture, or be forced outside, the Machaton range. To the east lies the Kruger National Park with many prides of lions of its own: no chance there of finding a range of their own on which they could begin to assemble a new pride. To the north and south are other Timbavati prides, each with their own fiercely protective males. The only other alternative is southwest, toward the Drakensberg Mountains. But there lies the greatest danger of all: the guns of the farmers who think of all lions, regardless of their coloring, as vermin – a threat to their cattle and little more.

There is a man in the area who's actually been known to lure the lions toward his fence by playing a tape recording of lions roaring. When they approach to investigate, he shoots them.

Whenever I found lions' spoor near this man's land, I used to set up my own tape recordings of lions roaring and try to lure them away in the opposite direction. It's extraordinary how well it works: they will often come right up to the jeep to see what's going on.

Another cruel threat are the trophy hunters. A white lion skin would be quite a conversation piece stretched out on somebody's living room floor or above a fireplace. A black-maned lion skin fetches about 600 rand (nearly $1,000); even an ordinary lioness skin is worth between 200 and 300 rand. I imagine you might be able to get as much as a couple of thousand rand for a white lion skin, well over $3,000.

And there's nothing to stop a relentless hunter from stalking and claiming such a trophy. Once they are outside the sanctuary of the reserve, the lions are unprotected by law.

The chances of Tombi surviving in the wild seem a little less grim. When lionesses reach maturity, they are quite often allowed to remain in the pride in which they were born. So far Tombi's unique coloring doesn't seem to have aroused any hostility among the other lionesses, so it is likely that she will continue to be accepted.

But if the other lionesses in the pride were to reject her or she turned nomadic for any other reason, her coloring would make her every bit as vulnerable as Temba.

In the meantime, the white cubs must survive the usual

dangers of growing up in a pride. So far Tabby's trio have been luckier than most, but there are many hazards ahead.

I thought over and over again about implanting an electronic device under Tabby's skin or fitting her with an electronic collar so that she and her cubs could be kept under close surveillance. They could thus be helped over any serious illness or injury, as Temba was at one stage when we found him limping badly, for what reason we just don't know. For five days, until he was fit again, we kept feeding the subgroup with impala that I'd shot. Usually the meat was immediately snatched up by the Musketeers, but eventually the young cubs got their share. If we hadn't done this, there was a grave danger that the pride would have moved on without him, leaving him defenseless in the bush. On another occasion, after we lost sight of them for a few weeks, we found the cubs looking emaciated and again provided them with a kill. By now we were fairly proficient at finding them, but there was still too much of an element of luck about it. An electronic tracking device could have removed all this uncertainty.

Starvation and the related risk of being fatally injured by older lions on a kill appear to pose the greatest threat to the cubs, now that they have grown out of the dangerous early stage. If there isn't enough to go round, the cubs might either go hungry or try to sneak a couple of bites when their elders and betters aren't looking. That's when they risk receiving a savage or perhaps even fatal blow, because feeding lions can be vicious.

The one time that I found Tabby's cubs alarmingly thin, Temba, always the adventurer, had a nasty gash on his muzzle. Seeing his ribs thrusting out like ridges on a sand dune, I made a confident guess that he'd stuck his nose into the dinner of one of his elders, and had got well and truly clouted for it.

I'd seen Temba try to jump his place in line at least twice previously. But the rebukes he received then from one of the Musketeers were only playful pats compared with the thrashing he got this time. My own guess is that the culprit was that unabashed disciplinarian, Achilles.

CHAPTER SEVEN

Living Dangerously

LIKE THE CUBS, WE OURSELVES WERE never really out of danger at this period.

Charlotte was helping out at Sohebele, then the one game-viewing lodge in the area. Sohebele is a camp like most of the others but it has been considerably enlarged to accommodate tourists, and enhanced, if you happen to look at it that way, with such amenities as electric lighting, a bar and a swimming pool.

Because of her childhood experiences in the bush, Charlotte had developed her own instinct for survival. It's just as well, for working at Sohebele exposed her to some extremely hazardous situations.

To get there involved a seventeen-mile drive through the thick of the bush – at least an hour's journey right through the middle of the Flop Ear pride's range. The drive home was even more harrowing, for it was usually made in the dark.

In general, Charlotte enjoyed driving in the evenings; we all did. There is a magic about the bush as the light dims and then fades altogether, and the warm night air is suddenly filled with the shrieking of the cicadas, known in this part of the world as Christmas beetles because it is at Christmas, our midsummer, that their shrill chattering reaches its crescendo. Along the track, shadows move silently among the trees and the headlights keep picking up the reflections from countless pairs of startled eyes – impala, kudu, steinbok. Sometimes, in a clearing, you see a hyena loitering to stare for a moment at the jeep before scuttling off into the shadows. And always, just as a small boat trails a phosphorescent wake, the jeep would be followed by squadrons of darting points of light, fireflies.

Charlotte worked at Sohebele for almost three months and made that thirty-four mile drive every day, usually in an open jeep. The variety of wildlife that she came across during these drives was staggering. She saw a newborn zebra and wildebeest only a few minutes old. And she saw snakes. One day a spitting cobra, which can blind you by spitting in your eyes from ten feet away, reared up in front of the car, threatening her.

There is no question that driving at night through lion country in an open jeep without a gun is highly dangerous. She was often terrified, but she loved it.

Most days Charlotte took Tabs and Gracie with her. One evening as they were driving home through the remotest part of the bush in a jeep provided for her by Sohebele, the engine suddenly died. (Our own Austin 1100, predictably, was broken down at the time.) Nothing she could do would get the car started again.

They couldn't just sit in the jeep, because they were

right in the center of the Flop Ear pride's range as it happened, and as Charlotte herself put it: "They're not nice lions at all, that pride. Nobody's very keen on them." She was worried that some or all of the fifteen lions might arrive and decide to get into the open jeep to investigate.

The safest thing, she thought, would be to start walking, before it got too dark. So they walked, Charlotte, Tabs and Gracie, all singing at the top of their voices. They sang Afrikaans songs, Shangaan songs, pop songs, whatever came into their heads. They didn't feel a bit like singing, any of them, but Charlotte's idea was to make sure that anything that might be lurking in the bush would know they were there.

They must have walked for a mile and a half, which is quite a distance when it's getting dark and you're walking in the bush with animals all around you. Finally, they came to the camp of Aniel, the local caretaker. He gave Charlotte a blanket, and she and Tabs and Gracie prepared to spend the night there.

While they were resting up, Aniel went out in the bush with two or three friends, all singing every bit as lustily as Charlotte and her crew, and for the same reason. They made their way to Sohebele to tell Rod Owen, who runs the camp, what had happened. Rod drove over to Aniel's later that night, and drove everyone home.

On another occasion, when Charlotte was driving the blue Austin 1100, using the main roads because it wouldn't go through the bush (a longer drive, but a slightly safer one) the car broke down at the Acornhoek turnoff. She and Tabs and Gracie decided to walk back to Vlak, at least an hour away on foot. They'd got about halfway back when Gracie suggested that they should all climb into a tree for the night.

They may have been on the main road, she reasoned, but it was still dangerous lion country and fences don't keep the lions in. They were preparing to climb into a tree when someone in a car came along and offered them a lift. That's a chance in a million on that road in the middle of the night, and it saved them from an uncomfortable and anxious experience.

The following day the people at Sohebele lent her a land rover to tow the Austin back to Sohebele to have it repaired. So at ten o'clock the next evening when she finished work, Charlotte drove the land rover back to the spot where the Austin had broken down. As well as Gracie and Tabs, she had with her a young Englishman named Mike who was staying at Sohebele and had agreed to go along to steer the Austin.

They set off, Charlotte driving the open land rover, with Tabs and Gracie sitting beside her, and Mike at the wheel of the helpless Austin, dragging behind.

When they came to a dry riverbed, they had to stop. Not only was the Austin's engine driven into the ground, but the brakes were gone as well. The only way Charlotte could get the car safely through the riverbed, which was a pretty steep incline, was to let it go down with its front bumper resting on the back bumper of the land rover, so that it could use the land rover's brakes and four-wheel drive to keep it under control. They had stopped to bring the two vehicles together to negotiate the incline, when suddenly they saw a whole sea of glowing eyes coming toward them, reflecting in the headlights of the land rover. At first Charlotte thought they were impala. But they weren't. They were fifteen lions, all running straight at the land rover – the whole bad-tempered Flop Ear pride.

Charlotte stopped the car, leaped out, pulled Tabby and Gracie out after her, and they all piled into the little Austin with Mike. Just as they shut the doors of the Austin, the lions came around past the headlights of the land rover and she could see them clearly. The lions immediately began to climb all over the land rover, and then they started sniffing around the Austin, literally towering over the tiny car. Naturally, the windows of the Austin wouldn't shut properly – no part of any car I've ever had works for very long – and the lions were breathing their hot horrible breath right in through the window.

Then the lions began to push at the Austin causing it to rock on its springs, and Charlotte and Tabs got a fit of the giggles. It was so terrifying, the only thing they could do was laugh about it.

The lions sniffed around the car for a full hour and then cleared off. At least they appeared to clear off. Charlotte couldn't be certain, because they couldn't see anything in any direction except dead ahead in the headlights of the land rover. They couldn't tell by listening, either, because lions make very little noise.

They waited for a while, then cautiously she put an arm out, and then a leg out, and they coughed and talked and made a lot of noise, and nothing happened. Suddenly she jumped out, dashed to the land rover, started it up, and headed for Sohebele, towing the Austin behind. Making that decision to run for the land rover was, she says, the worst moment of her whole life.

On another occasion I was making biltong at Vlak, vast quantities of it. Realizing that I had a big job on my hands in preparing the biltong, Charlotte promised to be home from work early to help me. When she finally arrived, I took one look at her and knew immediately that she had had yet another close call.

She had gone off to Sohebele that morning in one of their land rovers as the Austin was still giving us trouble. Poor Mike, who hadn't yet learned his lesson, once again volunteered to accompany her home so that he could drive the land rover back to Sohebele. Off they went and somewhere along the way to Vlak they came out of a clump of trees and found an enormous elephant standing right in the middle of the track. Charlotte reversed smartly – right smack into an anthill – and suddenly saw a whole pride of lions on the track behind her. She shot off into the bush at about fifty miles an hour bouncing over rocks and trees, through the scrub, until she was about a hundred yards from the track. There she stopped and waited.

Eventually the elephant ambled off and joined two others. The lions came forward a bit toward the jeep, but they were really far more concerned about the elephants. She was thus able to get back onto the track and drive on.

One day when Charlotte was on her way to work she came across some spoor that seemed to be heading toward a place we called Wisteria Creek. Thinking that the tracks probably belonged to our pride, she decided to turn around and find me. I was out in the jeep following one of the lion's roads, and she managed to locate me by retracing my tread marks. I headed off toward Wisteria Creek, and Charlotte set off again to Sohebele. As usual, Tabs and Gracie were with her.

Not long after she had left me, one of the front wheels of her land rover fell off. The day was extremely hot, over 100° – and there was no shade anywhere near them. Charlotte decided to send Gracie back to the camp on foot. It was a long walk for her, but Charlotte couldn't risk going along with her; it would have been too much for Tabs in that heat.

Gracie trudged back, picking up the wheel nuts that had fallen off the car as she walked, and finally found me in the bush on her way to Vlak. It was lucky she found me, because apart from the danger, it's not advisable to sit out in an open jeep in the sort of scorching heat you often get down here in November.

On another day when I was out on foot looking for the lions, Charlotte heard our pride roaring not far from the camp. Feeling that I would be disappointed if she didn't tell me, she took our jeep (and Tabs and Gracie, naturally) and set out to try and find me.

They hadn't got very far from Vlak when she got a flat tire. Needless to say, the jack wasn't working, so she tried digging a huge pit under the wheel, hoping to be able to change the tire that way. She kept on digging and digging . . . and in no time at all the jeep had fallen into the hole. It was getting dark and a light rain had started to fall. In the end, the three of them ran all the way to Vlak in the pouring rain, without a gun and with lions all around, leaving the jeep lying on the side of the road at an alarming angle.

One thing you learn in the bush is that there is a terribly narrow division between life and death. Often it's your life or the animal's, it's as simple as that.

Snakebites are the biggest danger of all in the bush, though we've all been very lucky so far. Apart from the spitting cobra, there are several types of mamba in this area, and if you're bitten by a black mamba, you've got exactly ten minutes to live. We always keep a supply of serum in the camp, and normally carry some out with us in the jeep whenever we go into the bush.

A friend of mine who didn't take the latter precaution was bitten by a black mamba not far from his camp. He got into the jeep and drove back as fast as he could. By the time he got there he was in such a nervous state that when he tried to open the vial of serum to inject himself, he broke it and spilled the whole lot on the floor. A few minutes later he was dead.

Tabs, even at her young age, has been exposed to death. She loves impala, particularly baby impala, but she is quite prepared to accept that we have to kill them for food, and she's not the least bit squeamish about watching us butchering them.

She had a baby warthog called PP (Pathetic Pig). Initially she had two. One of the trackers found them in the bush and brought them back to Tabs for pets. One died immediately, but the other one, PP, became a devoted friend and followed Tabs everywhere, even to the toilet. Unfortunately, it, too, became ill, with an ailment that Tabs called "dripply poo" (diarrhea). We did everything we could for the animal, including taking it to the hospital at Acornhoek for treatment. There's no way a hospital in America or England would ever look at a pet which also happened to be a wild animal, but because the staff knew us they did their best for PP. But to no avail.

Even the ordinary business of bringing up a child can be hazardous in the bush. Apart from all the standard ailments that children are subject to, there is always the danger of fever caused by insects. The nearest doctor is in Hoedspruit, though we could also telephone the resident doctor in the Kruger National Park for advice. In an emergency, though, the bush telephone could be a slow and uncertain means of communication.

Tabs did get tick bite fever once, and we had to take her all the way to Phalaborwa, a good three and a half hours' drive away. She was hospitalized for ten days. As we didn't want to leave her there on her own and couldn't possibly drive back and forth every day to see her, we simply camped on the hospital grounds, sleeping in the open beside the jeep. I don't think the hospital authorities were too pleased about this, but they didn't seem to know what to do about it. It wasn't a situation they had ever encountered before.

In ten days Tabs had completely recovered. She came straight out into the bush with us to spend the night sleeping in the jeep in the middle of the Machaton range, as we often did at this stage.

That night the three of us were fast asleep when Charlotte suddenly woke up and whispered: "I hear breathing." It was Agamemnon, less than three yards away. He'd come across the jeep and was just standing there looking at it. We could hear his hoarse, throaty breathing. He sniffed around for a few minutes and then was gone, as silently as he had come.

In the beginning Tabs was sometimes a bit nervous around the lions, but on this occasion she didn't seem at all worried. By now she had come to accept them as part of our everyday life; as my job, in fact.

And she accepts all the dangers and discomforts involved in living in the bush. If she gets a thorn in her foot, she doesn't come limping to Charlotte, she simply sits down and removes it herself.

She wasn't even unduly upset when we were charged by an elephant not long ago. I was driving the jeep and Tabs was in the back with Charlotte and another tracker, Mandaban. Something made them look around behind them and they saw an enormous elephant with his trunk raised, coming straight for the car. I was so intent on relighting my pipe that for a few seconds I didn't grasp the urgency of the situation. I hadn't seen the elephant because they were blocking my view to the rear.

When Mandaban finally got the message through to me, I stepped on the gas and went right down the nearest riverbed and up the other side, disregarding the fact that the jeep had no brakes at all at this stage. The elephant didn't bother to follow us once we got out of his path. He stayed over on the far side of the riverbed, flapping his ears and wildly waving his trunk.

It was frightening, but only momentarily so. It was all part of living in the bush.

ABOVE: Tabby was always very affectionate with her cubs and never showed the slightest sign of preferring Vela, the tawny one.

NEXT SIX PAGES: The cubs at play. It isn't difficult to pick out the various games like Pick-Up Sticks or Follow the Leader. The games of young lions can be roughly divided into two groups: those that simulate actions that lions use when killing their prey (jumping on Tabby's back, for example) and actions that they use when asserting themselves in the pride. Note how thin the cubs are in several of the pictures; this was one period when we were obliged to kill impala to feed them.

The face of a lion when food is in the offing. The lionesses have
made a kill, and from their growls the pride lions know where
to go, and know too that they will get "the lion's share."

When they make a big kill, lions eat an enormous amount of meat.
I've seen Agamemnon so full that he can hardly stand; he's
panting heavily, the saliva is dripping from his jaws, and he's
extremely uncomfortable.

If there is meat around, the lions will eat and eat until they are completely gorged. They can then last about a week, if they have to, without another meal. But the cubs have to take their chances.

The young cubs, like Temba, have to dart in and grab what they can, risking a cuff from one of the older lions if they prove too daring, and retiring as soon as possible (OVERLEAF) to a safe distance to enjoy the fruits of their audacity.

ABOVE: You can see from the way Temba and Tombi's ribs are showing through that the cubs have had a tough time. This is another occasion when I felt obliged to feed them. If I hadn't, the pride would almost certainly have deserted them and they would have starved. Temba – always the adventurer – had a nasty gash on his muzzle. Seeing his ribs thrusting out like sand dunes, I guessed that he'd stuck his nose into the dinner of one of his elders and had got well clouted for it.

RIGHT: The face of a young lion after the feast.

Almost from birth, lions are carnivorous; and whether they happen to be white or tawny, their life soon develops into a regular routine of sleeping, hunting, eating, and sleeping again.

Chapter Eight

Living Lion Style

By EARLY JANUARY THE HEAT was intense as the grass was lush. Pans of water gleamed like broken mirrors across the landscape, and the grazing and browsing animals wandered far afield and thrived. The lions had to travel a good deal further and work a lot harder for a living and, in turn, it became much more difficult for me to find them.

One moonless night I sat outside the camp with pipe, candle, compass, aerial photographs, pen and notebook, and a teakettle on the fire nearby. I wanted to record lion roars. In all, I have now collected more than 160 nights of roar data.

The first roar came five minutes before midnight, followed almost immediately by another.

Achilles and Agamemnon: they almost always roared in concert, and by now I could usually identify their performance because Agamemnon has a most distinctive roar. A male lion's roar begins low in his chest and wells up, exploding into a bellowing roar followed by a series of loud grunts, often as many as thirty. The grunts seemed to sound something like the word *gum* (the bushman's word for lion, in fact), with a very gutteral *g*. Often Agamemnon's penultimate grunt was much longer than the others.

That night, in a little more than four hours, I logged thirty-three roars. They came from at least four well-separated groups of lions up to three miles apart.

Then, around five A.M. there came a single roar that sounded fairly close to the camp. This was followed by a lot of snarling and growling that could mean only one thing – a kill.

Quickly I took a compass bearing and jumped into the jeep. Just before setting out, I'd heard the two big males roaring a long way from the kill.

Generally, the male lions would find out about a kill from the roaring and snarling and growling of the females of the pride and they would make their leisurely way to it, confident that as soon as they arrived they would be offered what has come to be known as "the lion's share."

In the faint light of the false dawn I drove straight through the bush and ten minutes later found the kill. The victim was again a wildebeest, brought down on the ecotone.

Six lions were wrestling over it – Golden and Tabby, and Golden's four teenagers, the Three Musketeers and Suzie Wong. A few paces away, watching enviously from the dewy grass, were Temba, Tombi and Vela.

Day was breaking almost directly behind the lions. Off to one side a lone hyena waited respectfully. To the other side a pair of jackals, less respectful, kept trying to dart in.

Temba decided to try his luck, but one of the Musketeers jumped on him with a warning snarl. Instantly, Tabby left her position at the kill and led her cubs away to a safer distance.

The wildebeest had almost been demolished when, away to the left, we heard a single low roar – Achilles. Only a hundred yards away, and for once without Agamemnon. Since the last roar I'd heard, he'd traveled almost two miles to get to the kill.

Now only fifty yards off, Achilles began to strut. Head up, chest out, he approached with the measured gait of a grenadier.

Seeing him, young Suzie Wong slunk away. When he was within ten paces, her brothers followed suit.

Only five paces from the carcass now, he stopped, uttered a single short growl, and resumed his measured gait. Instantly the other lions left the kill and ran off into the bush.

The sun rising behind him, Achilles stood over the carcass. He lifted his head and roared so loudly that the jeep vibrated. His breath came in puffs of steam. He roared again, then bent to sniff at the tangle of skin and bones.

Arrogantly, as though to indicate that what was left was not worthy of his attention, he sauntered off to rub his cheeks and urinate against a nearby bush, marking the place out as his territory. . . .

We had a couple of visits from photographers and film crews around this time, for inevitably the news of the existence of our white lions had begun to leak out.

It wasn't always easy to find the lions at a day's notice, especially during the rainy season, but usually an all-night vigil with books and candles in the jeep, during which I could trace Achilles and Agamemnon by their roars, led to the re-discovery of the pride. And on one occasion, it led to our finding the males in an unforgettable setting.

In the soft light of early morning they lazed on open sand with Golden, the Musketeers and Suzie Wong. Soon the sound of a waterbuck plunging through a nearby bed of reeds sent Golden off on an exploratory stalk. A cold breeze began to blow and, perhaps with shelter rather than water-buck in mind, the Musketeers trailed into the reeds.

Achilles rose to join the procession. As he paced purposefully away, I knew I couldn't simply let him slip from view — not with three eager telephoto lenses still trained on him. When he was ten or fifteen yards from the reeds, I made an effort at communication by trying to mimic a lion's call. Pitch and volume must have been right. Achilles stopped. He turned broadside on to us, feet together, great maned head high, tail curved. He listened intently.

With the trees and reeds behind him blurred by the long-focus lens, he made a superb calendar portrait, and the cameras clicked and rolled. Then, hearing nothing further, he continued his march and was swallowed up by the reeds.

Next Agamemnon, always the last to stir, was on his way. "Try it again," one of the cameramen urged me. Hearing my low imitation of lion cubs, the father of Temba, Tombi and Vela turned to face the jeep. He seemed even more intrigued than Achilles had been.

"Here he comes." We said it almost in unison as the enormous maned head advanced. Agamemnon strode straight toward the jeep.

"Make that sound again, and you'll have him right in here with us," someone whispered. I kept my mouth shut, and Agamemnon prowled past so close that we could almost have touched him. His burning yellow eyes were fixed on a clump of bushes beyond the jeep, and he looked rather puzzled when he found no lions waiting there. Quickly he sprayed the shrubbery, and having left his "calling card," sauntered off behind us.

Beneath a great old tree he paused to cast one more look at the place where he thought he'd heard a lion's call. Then he, too, went off into the gently rustling reeds.

To understand lions, you first have to look at the species upon which they prey; then at the trees and shrubs and grasses on which their prey feed. And to understand these, you have to get to the root of the matter, literally – to soils, nutrients and micro-organisms.

To put it another way, the number of lions and other predators in any given location is controlled primarily by the number of prey. These, in turn, are controlled by their habitat – by the availability of food and water, the nature of the grass and other factors.

During the period that I was observing the Machaton pride, their prey consisted almost entirely of the following animals: blue wildebeest (about 48 percent), giraffe and impala (about 12 percent each); kudu (10 percent); zebra and warthog (about 8 percent each); and waterbuck (2 percent).

According to Schaller's study of a pride in an East African game reserve, buffalo comprised about 62 percent of the lions' kill. There are almost five hundred Cape buffalo in the Timbavati Reserve and one herd of about two hundred is regularly within the Machaton pride's range. Yet to my

149

knowledge not a single buffalo has ever been killed by the Machaton lions. This demonstrates that the habits of prides vary widely in different regions. For example, all Machaton kills during the period of my study were made at night, yet in the adjoining Kruger National Park, lions have often been seen to kill by day.

It's interesting, too, that the Machaton lions steer well clear of elephants, but show no fear of rhinos. Animals only fear the known, not the unknown. Elephants are a known danger, and so the lions avoid them. I've seen Tabby lead her cubs quickly and almost furtively away, closely followed by Agamemnon, whenever elephants came bursting through the trees. On one occasion, however, I saw the lions with rhinos, recently reintroduced to the area after eighty years, and their reaction was quite surprising.

Late one afternoon Tabby and her brood, accompanied by Dimples, were lying on open sand near the Machaton when two rhinos, a bull and a teenager, appeared about two hundred yards away. They came snuffling and shuffling downwind toward the lions, pausing now and again to crop the short grass. Almost immediately the lions became aware of the rhinos. Tabby and Dimples both sat up for a brief look, then slumped to the ground and went back to sleep, obviously quite unconcerned.

Not so Temba, Tombi and Vela. All three immediately began to "stalk" the rhinos. Flattening their ears and creeping along on their stomachs, they moved from bush to bush. Still the rhinos advanced. With their poor eyesight they had no inkling that the lion cubs, two white and one tawny, were tracking them through the bush.

The cubs' behavior was not surprising. Unaware of any danger, they were merely playing a game. But I was amazed at

Tabby's reaction. Not even when her cubs were more than fifty yards away from her, and well within a quick thrust of those highly lethal rhino horns, did she seem to show any concern. Once in a while she'd open her eyes, take in the situation, and then drop off to sleep again.

Does this indicate that the "race memory" of animals is relatively short? That the instinctive fear which lions are believed to have felt for a dangerous and formidable enemy had disappeared during the eighty years that rhinos had been absent from this area? It is possible, of course, that lions never had any deep-seated fear of rhinos, but we have no way of knowing for certain.

By the same token, some people believe that, in time, lions may develop an instinctive fear of man's vehicles, since in some places they are constantly hunted from jeeps. If so, this would pose new generations of game wardens and wild-life experts with an almost insoluble problem, because it is not possible to approach lions on foot closely enough to study their behavior. It could happen, but on the evolutionary time scale it would probably take thousands of years to develop such an instinctive fear – certainly nothing that could be described as a race memory.

People often ask me why the Machaton lions always hunt at night. There is a theory that it's because people used to shoot lions in this area when there were some cattle here. The idea is that the lions started to hunt at night because it was safer for them then; there was less chance of their being shot.

But this is totally illogical because it's far easier to shoot a lion when he's resting in the sunlight than when he's hunting. Lions that hunt at night are actually far more vulnerable because they sleep so much during the day. What people don't realize is that most lions, probably as many as 80 percent, are nocturnal.

From the observations I've made, it appears that temperature plays a tremendously important part in influencing lions' behavior patterns. I have taken the breathing rates of these lions under all sorts of conditions and found that it can vary from 120 times a minute in the heat of the day to about 12 times a minute in the cool of the evening. My belief is that they are mainly nocturnal hunters because it's easier for them to be active when it's cooler. They'll hunt in daylight on the Machaton when it rains, or on an overcast windy day, so it looks as if there's a purely physical explanation behind it.

There's another prevalent theory about lions and other predators that needs to be challenged. This is the belief that if you want to increase the number of wildebeest or impala on your land the best way to do it is by shooting the predators that feed on them. I know a man quite near here, just outside the Timbavati Reserve, who openly boasts that he's recently shot eight cheetah because they were eating all his impala. He believes that by killing the cheetah he'll increase the number of his impala. In reality, the only thing he's succeeded in doing is to reduce the number of cheetah by eight.

There is no evidence that predators can seriously affect the overall numbers of prey animals except in particular instances, as when a species of predator is deliberately introduced into an area in which it has not naturally evolved. The mongoose, for example, was introduced into Jamaica in the 1870s in an effort to keep down the rats on the sugar plantations. Unfortunately, as rats are nocturnal and the mongoose hunt during the day, the two never encountered each other. And instead of ridding the island of rodents, the mongoose wiped out all the ground-nesting birds.

The very fact that any species of predator still exists today is proof that it has evolved in such a way that it cannot seriously limit the number of its prey. If it did, it would have become extinct. Many species of predators that have become extinct could have disappeared for this reason: because they became so efficient at hunting their prey, they wiped out their own means of subsistence, their own food supply.

This doesn't apply only to predators. If the wildebeest in any area eat all the grass, then the wildebeest will wipe themselves out in that area. Similarly, if the lions in any one area eat all the wildebeest and other game on which they prey, they too will wipe themselves out.

There are people who believe that man is well on the way to doing just that – contributing to his own extinction by destroying the very environment on which he depends for his continued existence. I think I would have to agree.

We have thousands of impala here, thirteen thousand at the last count. We know the numbers of game fairly precisely because each year the Department of Nature Conservation does a game count from the ground, taking a strip of land at a time, with teams of men walking or driving along the edges of each strip and double-checking the number of animals encountered. In 1976 we also did a helicopter count, flying on a grid system and counting all the animals seen from both sides of the helicopter on each sweep. There was a close correlation between the results achieved by these two methods.

In 1964 we had a drought and the reserve lost 40 percent of its impala population. Not through lack of water – there were adequate supplies of pumped water for the animals to drink; but because the lack of rain destroyed the vegetation and the animals starved. This is what primarily limits game numbers: the state of the habitat.

If you want to increase the number of impala or wildebeest or any other prey animal, the only way to do so is to improve the habitat – by providing more of what the animals need to live on.

And if you improve the habitat so that there are more impala, theoretically you are providing more food for the lions and other predators, so that you would logically expect an increase in the number of lions. But their numbers don't vary greatly from year to year. The high cub mortality, the system of throwing out the young males, the eventual defeat of the pride males by younger, more vigorous lions – in other words, their whole, complex social mechanism as it has evolved over the centuries – results in a stable population of lions in any one given area.

This is assuming, of course, that man, the ultimate predator, does not intervene.

I cannot see how lions in a reserve like Timbavati could ever breed to the point where they would become a problem to other species. Yet this is a very widespread idea, and not only in the bush. I'm trying to destroy this notion because we are losing predators all over the world through sheer ignorance of this basic fact of life.

Even man, over all the millions of years that he has existed alongside wildlife, did not succeed in wiping out more than a few species until the population and technological explosions of the last two centuries. In this period, so much irreparable damage to the environment has been done that in an effort to salvage something of the splendid diversity that life used to offer, a few enlightened people and governments have started fencing in huge tracts of whatever unspoiled terrain they can still find.

Behind these fences wildlife can survive, but only with man's help and surveillance. The environment in which the animals live is no longer a natural one. It has been artificially created and life within its confines can be maintained only by artificial means – by means of the new science of wildlife management.

CHAPTER NINE

A Question of Environment

ONCE UPON A TIME IN THIS part of Africa there was a complete natural ecosystem. There were no roads, no fences, no cities or towns. The animals evolved at their own pace and in their own way, each species finding a niche for itself in the scheme of things. And, by one method or another, they helped to sustain the others, each species controlling its own population growth and in some cases limiting those of other species so that a perfect balance was achieved and maintained for millions and millions of years.

When the bush got too thick and there was too little grass available for the animals that required it, a flash of lightning would start up a bush fire which would wipe out acres of scrub and allow fresh grass to grow.

When there was a drought, the animals would migrate westward toward the Drakensberg Mountains, where there have always been perennial streams.

Even the predators in the area never seriously competed with one another. The whole pattern of evolution has tended to minimize competition between the species.

The leopard, for example, hunts at night and seldom comes into the open by day. It hunts alone, almost entirely in the thick riverine bush, sometimes ambushing its prey from an overhead branch and taking the kill back up into the tree to feed on it. Like the lion, the leopard is a stalker, but it uses a different part of the terrain, and in general goes for smaller animals such as duiker, steinbok, baboon and impala. Occasionally a leopard will venture out of the riverine bush or go after something bigger, so that there's a slight overlap with the lion's requirements, but it is so slight that it does not constitute any significant competition.

The cheetah, the fastest of all cats, hunts quite differently. It's a daytime courser, relying heavily on its phenomenal speed. Cheetahs have neither the powerful jaws nor the extending claws of the lions and leopards. But this does not seriously handicap them. They are ideally equipped to outrun and kill their favorite prey, the impala. And because they rely on speed rather than camouflage to pull down their prey, they hunt almost entirely in the open plains.

The hunting habits of the Machaton lions place them almost exactly between the leopard and the cheetah. They hunt as a pride and avoid the thick bush that offers cover to the solitary, stealthy leopard. They also avoid the open plains that allow the cheetah to run down its prey unobstructed by trees and bushes. Instead they hunt almost exclusively at night and along the ecotone. The ecotone gives them enough cover for stalking and enough room to maneuver as a pride. In general they go for larger prey, animals big enough to feed a pride or a large subgroup. Wildebeest is their number one preference. But again, occasionally they will venture onto the plains and kill an impala, thus slightly overlapping the cheetah's territory.

To sum up, the whole scheme has developed in such a way as to minimize competition and produce what might be described as a very stable social system, far more stable than any of our own making.

A natural ecosystem is very much like a chain: each organism has its own role to play and is, in some way, linked to or dependent on certain others.

There is a small bird called the honey guide which works in perfect partnership with the honey badger, sometimes called the ratel. The honey guide has some method of detecting where beehives are situated and it leads the honey badger to them. The badger can get at the hive and eat the honey without being stung because it is equipped with tremendously thick skin around its neck which renders it impervious to bee stings – that is the way it has evolved over centuries. The badger eats the honey and leaves what it cannot eat or what it does not want to eat, the unhatched grubs of the bees. It is these grubs that the honey guide lives on.

Giraffes are covered in ticks, and there is a small bird called the ox-pecker that spends a lot of time perched on the necks of giraffes, because it lives on ticks and by eating them it is doing the giraffe a useful service as well as ensuring its own survival.

The aardvark makes holes in termitaria (anthills) in order to get at the termites, which form its staple diet. The holes it makes are then used, in turn, by warthogs who sleep in them at night. Sometimes the warthogs are ousted by the hyenas who use the holes as a safe place to drop their cubs. In the meantime, the surviving termites carry on their own highly

158

organized social existence in the untouched part of the anthill.

Incidentally, warthogs normally back into anthills: presumably as a precaution against predators. One evening Charlotte and I walked past an anthill in which we spotted an aardvark hole. I looked in and a face peered back at me – a face with tusks. I suspected that the animal would come rushing out, so I shouted a warning to Charlotte and jumped out of the way. The warthog came rocketing out, closely followed by another . . . and another . . . and yet another . . . We stood aside in disbelief as eight warthogs came bursting out of that den.

Warthogs, by the way, root up areas of grassland, exposing a certain type of corm, or bulb, on which the francolin live, so if there were fewer warthogs, there'd be fewer francolin. In turn, all sorts of creatures live off the eggs of the francolin and indeed the francolin itself.

Then there's the dung beetle. By some mysterious form of chemical communication, this extraordinary insect can detect the presence of fresh dung. The beetles arrive in vast numbers on the scene, and lay their eggs in a patch of dung. Then they roll the dung into a ball with the egg in the center, and push and roll the balls of dung away to a safe place where they bury them.

In this way the dung beetles break up the dung and spread it through the earth so that it can be absorbed and nourish the soil when the rains come. If there were no dung beetles the dung would bake hard in the hot African sun and remain on the surface in a form that could not be absorbed into the soil. In Australia they've actually started importing dung beetles from Africa to break up cattle dung and disperse it through the soil.

Presumably there is also a creature that lives on dung beetles, though I haven't encountered it yet. There's bound to be, because in an ideal ecosystem every niche is filled.

In this part of Africa there was once such an ecosystem – self-renewing, self-perpetuating and stable, with every organism contributing in some way, however tiny, to that overall stability.

Then man came along and started building cities and towns and roads and airstrips and fences, and the entire system collapsed. It can now only exist in isolated areas where it can be manipulated – and the manipulation that is needed to maintain and foster a natural ecosystem in an artificial environment is the science of wildlife management.

Consider the simplest, most basic need: water. In the early days if a severe drought occurred in one area, the animals would simply migrate to another area, where they could find water. They can't now, because of the fences, and so we have to provide them with water artificially.

When Timbavati was formed there was one natural perennial spring in the lions' range, but there are now a number of man-made dams: the Machaton Dam, the Ostrich Dam and the Elephant Valley Dam. Also, some of the natural pans are now windmill-fed; water is pumped up to them from boreholes, using wind power. Two of our lions' favorite watering holes, Piggy Dam and the natural marsh known as the Bulrushes, are windmill-fed. This is wildlife management at its most basic level. If you put up fences that prevent the animals from reaching natural sources of water, then you must provide artificial sources of water for them or they will not survive.

But wildlife management goes further and deeper than that. It is difficult to grasp the fact that if you want to conserve a species of animal in an area that's been fenced off, you must start by ignoring the animals; they'll breed up again in five years' time, given the right conditions. The habitat, not the animals, must be the prime consideration, because it is the habitat that largely controls the number of wild animals.

When the land was fenced off there was an immediate deterioration in the habitat which was reflected, paradoxically it seems, by an increase in the number of impala. Most varieties of antelope are selective in their eating habits; they can either browse or graze and will eat only certain types of grass or leaves. But impala are exceptions to this. They are both grazers and browsers, and will eat virtually anything that grows. So within the fenced area they soon eat everything available. In consequence the more-selective grazers suffer, being forced to roam further afield in search of what they need to live on, while the impala prosper.

In good years, when there is plenty of rainfall and consequently plenty of vegetation, there is enough for all the species. In 1964, however, during the severe drought, Timbavati lost many rare animals, such as the roan sable antelope. They died out as a result of the fence, which prevented their migration.

There's no point in trying to reintroduce a species to an area if you haven't first established what its specific requirements are. Then you must manage things in such a way that you improve the habitat so that it is capable of supporting the species. Once that has been done, the species can then be reintroduced. But to do all of this successfully, there must be more research into ecology. We've got to study these rare species in depth in areas where they still exist, and then manage the fenced-in wild to recreate these conditions.

My own attitude to the problem has changed fundamentally as a result of my studies in America. In wildlife management circles around the world, the traditional concept of preservation, which focused on saving the animals themselves, has now given way to an emphasis on conservation, which focuses attention on what really determines animal numbers – the habitat. If you lose a few animals here or there through snaring or poaching, or through some misguided character shooting cheetah because he thinks he's going to increase the number of his impala, or through some farmer notching up two hundred plus lions, it's disgraceful – but it's still not that significant. These actions have no long-term effect on the animal population. What we really need to concern ourselves with is the state of the environment.

And to get the environment, the habitat, into a state that will support the widest possible variety of life, you have to accept the need for culling.

Culling – it's still a controversial, hot-under-the-collar word to preservationists. The very idea of shooting wild animals to conserve them seems a contradiction in terms to many people. Yet modern conservationists know that in areas subject to periodic drought, surplus animals must be culled. In an artificial environment, culling cannot be left to predators, calf mortality rate and other natural causes.

It has been scientifically established that Timbavati at present has too many impala and giraffe. If some of them are not removed, the surplus, and many more as well, will surely die in the next drought, and before they die will have irreversibly damaged the habitat. During the drought in 1964, many thousands of impala and some three hundred giraffes slowly

162

starved to death here. If not regularly culled or "harvested," surplus animals, even in normal years, can wreck an environment by overgrazing or overbrowsing – usually to the detriment of other species as well. The overgrazed surface would be trampled loose, and precious topsoil that had taken a hundred years to build up would be washed away by the first heavy rains. Next, inferior vegetation would take over. If this in turn were allowed to be overgrazed, the ultimate result would be a desert.

At the moment there is a direct clash between conservationists and preservationists. The trouble is that landowners favoring preservation can wreck a whole scheme by saying they don't believe in culling and won't allow any shooting on their land. This prevents any planned effort at overall conservation. I'm not specifically referring to Timbavati here. Timbavati is only one of dozens of reserves, private and national, in southern Africa, and the people who run them are by no means united in their views.

The sad thing is that conservation cannot be approached piecemeal. If it's going to work at all, it must be instituted on a grand scale, and it must be done soon.

Otherwise it will be too late.

One of the wildlife management tools now being used in Timbavati and elsewhere is a scheme of periodic rotational burnings. This is one way of enforcing rotational grazing among the animals, something that happened naturally when there were no fences and when natural burns were not limited by roads and other man-made obstacles or by misguided men who put the fires out. We know that fire was an essential element in the natural ecosystem because, among other things, there are certain types of tree that bear seeds that will not germinate until they have been scorched by fire.

After the shrubs are burned away, there is a growth of new green grass that attracts a lot of game away from areas that are in danger of being overgrazed, areas that desperately need a rest if they are to recover. If you exclude fire, which has been part of the evolutionary pattern since the world began, you change the whole nature of the environment: it gets far more wooded, with too many trees and shrubs. This limits the amount of open grass, which in turn limits the number of grazing animals the area can support.

That was one of the first mistakes made by man when he started fencing off the wild: his tendency to exclude fire, probably for sentimental reasons. People used to worry about tortoises, ground-nesting birds and other wildlife that would inevitably get burned in a fire. But this pattern has been going on for millions of years. Fire hasn't wiped out tortoises in the past and it won't now. Perhaps it appears cruel to start a fire deliberately in which numbers of helpless animals will inevitably be destroyed. But nature, left to her own devices, is far more ruthless than man could ever be, and only by such seemingly ruthless methods can the environment be conditioned to continue to support all wild species.

When severe scrub encroachment occurs, you need a hot burn to get rid of it, and you can only achieve this by setting fire to the tall, dry grass. This in turn will destroy the scrub and open up whole new areas for grazing. We now burn to a planned pattern, usually up to four thousand morgen at a time. (A morgen is a land measurement used in this part of Africa. The word simply means "morning" in Dutch, and it's the amount of land that one man with an ox or a horse can plow in a single morning, a little over two acres.)

164

Without a scheme of regular burns, you get an excess of scrub and the land that still has grass on it goes to ruin through overgrazing. At that point there isn't enough long grass left for a hot burn, and there is no easy way that you can stop it from deteriorating still further.

Maintaining the balance is the essence of wildlife management. The ecological system existed and it worked perfectly well for countless millions of years. Now we've disturbed it, and the only thing we can do is to try to acquire some knowledge of how it worked and use every skill within our grasp to restore it to a state in which it will work again.

It is marvelous how efficiently the indigenous animals of Timbavati utilize the habitat. The giraffe is a top-level browser, and eats the leaves from the tops of the trees. The kudu is a mid-level browser, and eats leaves a bit lower down. The impala, by far the commonest of Timbavati's wild animals, is both a low-level browser and a grazer. Lowest of the browsers is the tiny steinbok.

Then come the purely grazing animals. The buffalo is the only grazer that can comfortably handle the thick strands of perennial grass. These it grazes and tramples down, opening up the lower levels of grass to other animals. Next in the grazing succession comes the wildebeest, which prefers a shorter, sweeter grass. Then the impala and so on.

Timbavati is trying to reintroduce some of the more selective grazers and browsers that disappeared when the fences went up and the impala demolished the leaves or grasses upon which they depended for their existence. A small herd of sable antelope is now being kept in a special fenced-off reserve about a mile square until there are enough of them, either through natural increase or further acquisition, to be released with some chance of survival. The theory is that the more that are released at one time, the greater their chance of survival.

Since the wild is now fenced in, it must be run by people who know something about wildlife management, people who are sensitive to the fact that management must be instituted on a large scale and on a scientific basis. It won't work if some of the landowners refuse to cooperate.

Take culling as an example. If all the owners agreed, we could cull regularly, just like harvesting a crop. This would not only improve the habitat for the species we cull and for other, rarer species, but it would also bring in a certain amount of revenue, which the reserve could then use for further wildlife management projects.

If impala are not culled on a regular basis, they wreck the habitat for themselves and others. When you cull them regularly, you solve this problem. You also have a remarkable product on your hands because every part of the animal can be sold: the meat; the hides; the bones; even the hooves, which are sent to Japan and made into gelatin for glue and other products. Most of the meat is made into biltong in local workshops. The scraps that are left over are made into sausages and the bones are sold for bonemeal. The skins are tanned and fetch between 8 and 12 rand ($12 to $18) a-piece, or they can be made into *karosses*, skin blankets, which are sold at a slightly higher price.

The revenue is then used to finance such operations as rescraping the firebreaks to make sure that they are effective, or carrying out a helicopter count of the animal population. Rotational burning schemes could also be supported by these funds. A big burn entails hiring about thirty men for a couple of days. On the first day they set the veld on fire and then stand watch to see that the fire doesn't get out of control. On the second day they have to cover the entire area again to check that there are no logs still glowing in a position where they could set fire to acres of bush that we don't want to burn. All of these are costly procedures.

At the moment we are limited at Timbavati in various ways. The people who make the biltong can cope with only twenty or so impala a night; and, as there's only a short period during the year when the climatic conditions are right for making biltong, this limits the extent of the culling operation, which in turn curtails the overall effectiveness of the conservation plan.

Ideally I'd like to see at least one of the private nature reserves in this part of Africa taken over as a research territory by one or more of the universities, in conjunction perhaps with the Department of Nature Conservation. Researchers in wildlife management from all over the world could have access to it, and the project could be financed partly from the proceeds of culling operations and partly perhaps from limited tourist use. In time the territory could even become a "pilot plant" where rare species could be bred up under controlled conditions and their precise habitat requirements carefully studied. In this way other areas of the wild could be restocked with some measure of success.

If even one of these private reserves could be run in this thoroughly scientific way, we would stand a much stronger chance of preserving at least a small part of the wild.

Man – there's the ultimate threat to all wildlife. If we can ever discover some acceptable way of controlling the sensitive balance between human interests and wildlife, then wildlife could survive. If we don't and we allow direct competition between the two in places like Timbavati, then the wildlife will inevitably vanish – as it has already done almost all over the world.

CHAPTER TEN

The Cubs Grow Up

ONE AFTERNOON I CAME UPON A "culling" attempt by a group of raw novices.

It was mid-December and an old bull giraffe was patrolling the belt of bush along the Mayembule, a tributary of the Machaton. Between him and the jeep there were over a hundred yards of low grass, dotted with still leafless shrub. Prostrate in the grass lay Tabby and Dimples, not the least bit interested in the old bull. But creeping toward the giraffe was a trio of diminutive lions.

Temba was in front, a wiggling white blob, startlingly conspicuous against the green. Vela was two bushes to his left, Tombi a bush further back. The giraffe watched their stalking efforts with ears cocked and eyes that seemed to bulge from his head. When the cubs were within fifty yards, he ambled a bit further on. Then he turned to look again. In his head, it seemed, a battle was raging between his obvious curiosity and his inborn wariness of lions.

When the cubs crept uncomfortably close, the giraffe retreated again. He covered the ground deceptively fast with an awkward prancing style, moving both left legs, then both right legs. For nearly an hour this comical game of hide and seek continued, the old bull moving just far enough up and down the river to keep the three little cubs guessing.

In this season of luxuriant growth, in fact through the whole year, one of the surest ways of locating Temba and Tombi was to scout regular lion roads and observe the giraffes. From its great height, a giraffe can see over much of the bush and spot animals that can't possibly be seen from the jeep. A preoccupied giraffe that wasn't browsing from the leaves of the trees or looking at the jeep itself, certainly one of the strangest and noisiest creatures along the Machaton, might well be watching the white lions.

About twenty times we saw giraffes staring intently at something and on approaching more closely found Tabby and her cubs. Only once did we ever see a giraffe looking at ordinary lions.

Late in March the cameramen paid us another visit. This time there were two: Mike Holmes, a freelance writer and still-life photographer who assisted me in photographing and recording the development of the white cubs in their early stages; and Mike Burts, a movie cameraman from Johannesburg.

For two full days we jolted and bounced in pursuit of pictures that are a wildlife photographer's dream. The jeep was so crammed with equipment, food and water that every change of position had to be carefully considered. Mike Burts stood head and shoulders out of the cage at the back, Arriflex camera on a tripod securely lashed into place.

170

Beside him sat Filori, a tracker. Beside me was Mike Holmes with three Kodachrome-loaded Nikons, one resting on a small sandbag which he was using as a make-shift tripod.

In the dew of early morning the plains were laced with spiderwebs. The spiders were after a number of insects – midges, flies, mosquitoes and butterflies – that flitted above the flats. One long-legged black and yellow spider had spun a magnificent web right across our path. As we approached, with the jeep's cage rattling fearfully, the two Mikes saw the spider gather up the lower part of the web – almost like a curtain being raised – and we passed safely beneath. Then it dropped its silky skein back into place again.

Filori was acting as game spotter, calling out the species we were seeing in matter-of-fact Zulu.

"*Inkonkoni!*" A lone wildebeest blundering through the scrub.

Then: "*Amadube!*" Several zebra cantering off in a dazzling retreat.

Soon we saw our first *impala* of the day – the name is also Zulu. A herd of about twenty-five of them came soaring across the road. Obviously no lions here. We turned and made toward the Machaton.

"Look out for vultures," I said as Filori and I scanned the soft sand of the alkaline flats. First for telltale shapes and colors under the shingayi. Then for tracks.

Not a sign. Not on that cold, gray Friday. Most of the next day was no different.

Knowing that in weather like this the lions often shelter in the riverine bush, we peered into the foliage along the river and into the tall grass. Still we saw nothing.

As we drove, the photographers were treated to the usual cavalcade of other wildlife: lesser hornbills and ground horn-

171

bills; carmine bee-eaters that dived to catch insects stirred up by the jeep; lilac-breasted rollers, secretary birds, Bataleur eagles, francolin, guinea fowl, warthog, rhino, buffalo, jackal, duiker, kudu, squirrels, baboons, a waterbuck family . . .

It was late in the day when, near a tributary of the Machaton, Mike Holmes happened to glance back. A young lion sat under a shingayi watching the departing jeep. It was one of the Three Musketeers. "The others must be in that thick stuff," I whispered, motioning to the tangle of trees along the riverbed. But they were closer. Only twenty yards away, almost obscured by tall grass, was the camouflaged but unmistakable head of another of Golden's offspring.

We could get no closer and it was nearly dusk. Besides, the white cubs were unlikely to be with the Musketeers and Suzie Wong; Tabby had so far kept them carefully out of range.

At least we'd have a starting point in the morning . . .

Back at camp that evening we heard lions roaring from three different places within a few minutes. We marked the direction of the roars carefully in the sand. Charlotte and I estimated the distances and took compass bearings, then plotted the approximate positions on the old aerial photograph.

Then we joined our guests for an open-air *braaivleis*, a bush-style barbecue in the *guma*, the circular, reed eating enclosure. A leadwood fire burning down to glowing embers in a sand pit gave a warm and cheerful light.

"I'm sure the white cubs are with the middle group," Charlotte announced with her uncannily confident instinct for the bush.

The following morning we had our usual difficulty in getting the jeep started – an ignition fault – but at last managed to get it going and left before breakfast. Fifteen minutes later we were at the place where Charlotte had predicted we would find the white cubs, and the jeep clattered up an incline.

"There they are! There they are!" Mike Burts whispered excitedly. "And the white cubs are with them."

Tabby and the cubs were walking obliquely away from us about sixty yards to the right. Off to the side were two half-grown lions, two of the Musketeers hobnobbing for the first time with Tabby's cubs.

The photographers were as amazed as we had all been at the whiteness of Temba and Tombi.

At six months the cubs were no longer the snowy white of their early days but they were still undeniably white, there was no mistaking that. They could only be described as white lions.

I felt confident now that they wouldn't turn tawny. Parts of the pelt that are darker on ordinary lions – like the ridge of the back or the tip of the tail – were now cream or a light dusty brown on Temba and Tombi. Elsewhere they were still as white as polar bears.

All too conscious of our earlier starter trouble, I was reluctant to turn off the ignition. If the lions moved off and we couldn't get the jeep moving again, we'd lose them. Or worse still, if the lions moved toward us . . .

Luckily Tabby chose to rest in the open for two precious minutes and, with the motor running, the photographers worked fast. Then the extraordinary family was on its way again, the cubs trotting contentedly along at Tabby's heels. This was yet another overcast day and, typically, the lions made for the river. We trundled along after them.

Just before reaching a thicket, Tabby stopped in three-foot grass. Tombi, who was nearest, squatted down beside her mother and suckled briefly. So, at six months, the cubs were still being nursed, despite the fact that we had seen them eating meat from their earliest weeks.

As the photographers were trying to get some clear shots of the cubs, I alerted them to the possibility of drama should one of the Musketeers venture too close to Temba, Tombi or Vela. Tabby was lying on her stomach and the cubs sat and paced, sat and paced. Temba and Tombi stood out clearly through the grass; Tabby and Vela were almost invisible. Briefly one of the Musketeers came into view in the background. At once Tabby stood up between him and her brood, baring her teeth and giving a low rumbling growl. Feigning nonchalance but taking the hint, the Musketeer stalked down to the riverbed.

Soon afterward, Tabby and the restless cubs followed and were gone. Not even the jeep could force its way through that barrier of trees. By the time we'd backtracked to the other side, the lions had vanished.

When we saw them next, they were again with the Musketeers. This was strange because up to this point, Golden, the leading lioness of the group, was always with her own cubs, the Three Musketeers and Suzie Wong. That was one fixed subgroup of the pride, and on many occasions this subgroup was accompanied by Scarleg, acting as nursemaid and helping Golden with the hunting. Sometimes the subgroup would be joined by the two pride males, Achilles and Agamemnon; and occasionally, when they were feeling sociable, Greta and Lona would put in an appearance.

When Tabby's cubs were about nine months old, Suzie Wong and the Musketeers joined up with Tabby's subgroup. It seemed that Golden had thrown them out, possibly because she was expecting another litter of cubs herself.

Prior to this, Tabby had always kept the Musketeers at bay, realizing that they constituted a menace to her young cubs. However, as soon as Temba, Tombi and Vela were old enough to look after themselves, she allowed the others to join her group, though she has always exercised complete dominance over them. Time and again I've seen and photographed them making submissive gestures to her.

Tabby and Dimples continued to do all the hunting. They had to. The Musketeers still haven't a clue about stalking, they're pathetically bad at it. They were virtually defenseless when they attached themselves to Tabby. But they'll have to learn fairly quickly because they are due to be thrown out altogether any time now, in three or four months at the most. It is probable that Suzie Wong, who has grown up into a very attractive young lioness, will stay on as part of the pride. I wouldn't be surprised if she mated with Achilles or Agamemnon anytime now. She is the daughter of one of them, obviously, but incest is not an uncommon feature of life among a pride of lions.

Indeed, it could be one explanation for the appearance of the white cubs.

I have no way of knowing how old Achilles and Agamemnon are. It is almost impossible to tell in the wild. If you examine Agamemnon's teeth through binoculars, you can see that they are well worn, so obviously he is not very young. Certainly he could be old enough to be Tabby's father or grandfather. Thus, if a white recessive gene exists among these lions and you have the situation of a father mating with his own daughter or granddaughter, the chances of the white strain appearing are naturally increased.

By now we knew the cubs quite well. Tombi, the white female, is very like her mother, extremely casual. She is much more timid than Temba, and like Tabby, not really interested in either us or the jeep. She just accepts us and, for the most part, ignores us.

Temba is constantly in trouble; he is always getting minor wounds and injuries. On a kill he blunders in without thinking and frequently gets a good sharp clip from one of the older lions. He's had a big wound, probably from a claw, right beside his nose. He has also injured his legs several times. Once he had a chunk missing from one of his hind legs. He's not so much aggressive as foolhardy, slaphappy even.

Vela, the tawny one, was a slow developer. In the early days he wasn't nearly as adventurous as the other two cubs, but he seems to have caught up with them and even to have overtaken them. He's grown into a very handsome, very spunky little lion, and he's got quite a respectable mane now, which is more than Temba can boast.

In this part of the world there are naturally maneless male lions as well as lions with black manes, blond manes, and rufous manes. In scrubby, thorny country, even normal lions tend to have less manes than lions in open country. I've seen bits of mane on bushes all along the lions' favorite routes and even on the lower parts of fences, where the lions have wriggled underneath.

Temba grew the beginnings of a slightly sandy-colored mane when he was about ten months old, but when it was nearly nine inches long it disappeared. It is possible that this has something to do with the fact that he is white – we just don't know. His mane may return, or it is possible that he may grow up to be a maneless lion.

ABOVE: This picture of Temba and Vela illustrates that at well over one year old the white lions of Timbavati were still very white – and showing no signs of turning tawny.

OVERLEAF: As the cubs grew up they retained many of the characteristics we had first observed in them, but there were changes. Temba (TOP RIGHT) grew the rudiments of a mane and then lost it again; Tombi (MIDDLE RIGHT) became very casual, like her mother Tabby; and Vela (LOWER RIGHT) lost his shyness and became a very attractive, spunky little lion.

FOLLOWING PAGES: Mostly we saw them in subgroups resting under the shade of shingayi trees (FAR RIGHT). When Tabby's cubs were about nine months old, the Musketeers joined up with her subgroup (TOP LEFT), but we often saw Tabby alone with the white cubs (BOTTOM LEFT).

Lions are extremely lazy animals. They believe in conserving their energy as much as possible, and rest up to sixteen or eighteen hours a day.

When they are not asleep, they stretch out comfortably in the shade. It is not until the cool of the evening (OVERLEAF) that they stir themselves and start to move about.

We crossed the river and suddenly we came upon four of the lionesses with a crop of new cubs. It was impossible to tell how many cubs there were, but one of them was white – every bit as white as Temba and Tombi, and only about six weeks old. We named the new white cub Phuma, which in Zulu means "to stand out" or "to be out of the ordinary."

As one of ten cubs born at roughly the same time, Phuma's chances of survival didn't seem very high, but she developed into a very healthy little lion cub with even more spirit than Temba and Tombi.

ABOVE: Phuma is now well past the perilous first period of a cub's life. She's very aggressive on a kill and often chases the other cubs off until she's had her fill.

OVERLEAF: With so many mouths to feed, a large subgroup (ten cubs and four lionesses) tends to hunt larger animals, such as giraffe.

In this extraordinary place, an oasis in a world of disappearing and endangered species, what appears to be a new strain of wild animals has suddenly appeared. The birth of Phuma raises the intriguing possibility that yet more white cubs may be born to the pride – and with man's help may be enabled to survive.

By this time we could find the lions relatively easily by simply driving out in the jeep and scouting around their favorite resting places. Nevertheless, I continued to walk the bush at this time with Mandaban, another tracker – partly to keep my hand in, as far as spooring was concerned, and mostly because I've never been able to get over the thrill of watching lions on foot. It's a completely different experience – not a bit like watching them from a jeep. You are in their world, on the same scale with them. Lions are the only animals in the world that give me this thrill.

Spooring itself is a fascinating activity. You can usually tell how recent a spoor is from the extent that it's been eroded away. This is dependent, of course, on the nature of the ground, the weather and various other factors.

Also, if you walk along a track following the spoor and there are no other fresh marks made by other animals on top of it, you can assume that not much time has elapsed since the lions walked there. The whole business is complicated, of course, by the fact that lions can scent you a very long distance away if you are approaching on foot, so if possible you have to keep downwind of them. You must also constantly be on the lookout for other clues. Eagles or vultures in the trees or circling overhead might indicate lions on a kill. Alarm calls from other animals could be an indication that there are lions about. Or an animal looking particularly wary and not looking at us: that could be another sign.

On one occasion recently, Mandaban and I were following spoor and had reached a point where we knew we were getting close to them. We split up and I inched forward carefully. Suddenly I caught a glimpse of white under a tree – one of the white cubs looking right at me.

This was a tense situation. The mother, Tabby, was

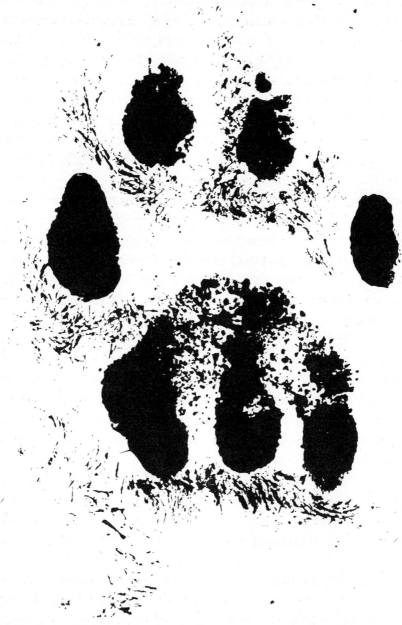

Artist's rendition of a fresh lion spoor

obviously still asleep somewhere nearby. If we happened to wake her, she would almost certainly charge; lionesses with cubs invariably do, if someone approaches on foot. The sensible thing would have been to withdraw quietly, then return later and watch them from the jeep.

But for a few minutes, I couldn't find Mandaban, and of course I couldn't call out for fear of awakening Tabby. When I did locate him, I discovered that he'd walked right past Tabby, within twenty yards of where she was still sleeping. He had stopped a bit further on and was looking at the two pride males, Achilles and Agamemnon, also fast asleep. They were clearly recovering from an enormous meal, fortunately, and didn't look as if they were likely to wake up in a hurry.

He withdrew quietly, without having seen either the white cubs, thirty yards to his left, or Tabby only twenty yards away from him. It was just sheer luck that the lioness didn't awaken.

Sheer luck, and the natural greed of lions.

For when they make a big kill, they eat enormous amounts of meat. I've seen Agamemnon so full that he can hardly stand; he's panting heavily, the saliva is dripping from his jaws, and he's obviously extremely uncomfortable. He doesn't move. He simply lies there, with a stomach like a balloon that's just about to burst.

If there is meat around, the lions will eat and eat until they are completely gorged. They can then last for about a week, if they have to, without another meal. This ability to gorge could be an evolutionary advantage in areas where food is scarce.

Here, of course, food is abundant all year round. But the tendency of the animals is to eat whatever is immediately available and make no provision for the morrow. In more northern climates, animals like squirrels store food against the possibility of a harsh winter, because if they didn't they might not survive. In this part of Africa, though, there is no need to plan ahead: the sun shines most of the time; there is no winter such as there is in most parts of the Northern Hemisphere; and there's normally plenty to eat.

One of the gaps that still exists in my study of the lions' behavior is data on the frequency with which they kill. I have recorded about a hundred kills, but I can't say for certain whether this even remotely approaches the total because I have no way of knowing whether I have seen them all. What I really need to do is to study the pride continuously, day and night, for several sample periods of about two weeks, spread out over a year. The longest continuous period I've ever been able to spend with my lions was five days, and that's just not long enough to give me a reliable index from which to work out the probable total number of kills.

With a selection of two-week periods spread out over a few months, or better still a year, I would have a reliable frequency index. I could then say that if the pride killed x wildebeest on average during six or eight sample periods, then in any given year, they are likely to kill y wildebeest. By combining this information with what I already know about their prey preferences, it should be possible to figure out exactly the impact they have on the prey species. This would help greatly when it came to working out a plan for a culling operation, because we would then be able to tell, with reasonable accuracy, how many of each species were likely to be culled by the lions. This is all part of the science of wildlife management.

One thing I have noticed is that the lions kill about twice as many impala rams as they do females. This could be because the males are more often found on their own. Antelopes like impala travel in herds for their own protection. A herd has more eyes and ears than a solitary animal and can spot a stalking predator very easily. Lone impala rams are much more vulnerable. But even if the lions and other predators killed nine out of ten males (which they certainly don't), it still wouldn't have much long-term effect on the overall numbers of impala because one male can serve thirty ewes.

When lions attack a herd of impala or wildebeest, as they are sometimes obliged to do when no stray males are available, they go for stragglers, the weaklings, often the old and sick animals, simply because they are easier to bring down. But in so doing, they are, in effect, contributing to the survival of the fittest.

As Schaller points out: "Predators are the best wildlife managers. They weed out the sick and old, and keep the herds healthy and alert."

CHAPTER ELEVEN

To Kill a Lion

IN JULY I WAS FORCED TO shoot one of the Musketeers.

I went out late one night because I hadn't seen the white lions for about three weeks. My stay at Vlak had come to an end, and I had been asked to take on the job of game warden for Timbavati on a temporary basis. But with my varied duties in that capacity, I simply didn't have time to keep track of the lions. Also, I was now based in a different camp, much further away from the lions' range.

In order to find them again as rapidly as possible, I decided to sleep out on the Plains where the lions normally hunt at night at that time of the year. I had Mandaban and a friend of his with me and we planned to spend the night in the back of an open pickup truck, listening for roars. We had to use the open pickup. There was no way that three adults would be able to sleep in the caged jeep.

But the lions weren't roaring that night and eventually we all dropped off to sleep. At about two in the morning,

Mandaban started to nudge me and whisper urgently in my ear. I woke up to find that the lions were all around us. We hadn't found them – they'd found us.

They were right on top of us: the Three Musketeers, Tabby, the two white cubs and Vela, and probably Dimples and Suzie Wong. It was a bright, moonlit night and we could see their heads, which were far higher than the level at which we had been sleeping.

Initially my instinct was to remain as quiet as possible and not do anything. But as the minutes ticked away, the situation became more and more terrifying. They were so close. If one of them had taken it into his head to leap aboard to investigate, we'd have been finished. Lying down as we were in the back of the open pickup, we were completely defenseless.

In the past I had always found that if I stood up suddenly in a situation like this, the lions would slink away immediately, just as they normally do when you approach them on foot. I decided that the safest thing would be to do just this. Then, as soon as they withdrew, we'd leap out of the back of the truck and run round to the cab. Inside the cab, at least we would have had some protection.

I whispered to the others to be ready to make a run for the cab and then stood up, making quite a noise in the process.

The lions all fled – except one of the Musketeers, who began by making a mock charge that landed him within six paces of the truck. I was still acutely aware of all the lessons I had learned from Jack. This was a moment to stand firm and exude confidence and force the lion to back away.

The trouble was that on this occasion I only had a small rifle with me, and there was no way that it would have stopped that Musketeer if he ever started to spring. I knew that, and I suppose he sensed something of my fear.

For what seemed like hours I stood there, the inadequate rifle cocked and pointed at him, the animal crouched in the position lions always adopt prior to a spring – front paws stretched out, head low on the ground, hind quarters slightly raised.

I didn't know for sure whether he was going to spring or not, but I couldn't afford to take the chance. If he had come at us, there was no chance at all that the rifle could have stopped him in mid-air. He would have landed right in the back of the pickup and would have taken at least one of us with him.

So I fired.

I've spent endless hours questioning myself about this and doubting my actions. Would he have sprung if I had held my fire for another second or two? Or would he have given up and slunk away into the bush? I just don't know. It was bad judgment going out without the proper gun; with a small gun you don't have the luxury of taking a chance. There were also two other lives involved.

So I fired.

I got him in the shoulder and he dropped. The gun didn't kill him instantly, as a big gun would have done, but he lost all interest in us immediately and his head dropped to the ground motionless. When we skinned him the next day, we found that he had a nasty festering wound near the base of his spine, which could have accounted for his aggressive behavior. I had known this lion for more than a year and a half; I had watched him grow up and had taken over sixty photographs of him and never felt even remotely threatened before.

I was extremely sick about the whole incident.

The fact that I was so desperately upset about shooting one lion in what really amounted to self-defense underlines the huge change that has taken place in man's attitude toward the question of shooting predators. I talked about this subject at length with a man called Gustav Battenhausen who had a camp here in the early 1940s, when killing lions was regarded as something of a lark.

When Battenhausen bought his farm in 1939, there were only three other landowners in the area. One of them, a man I'll simply call Jan, had a herd of about four hundred cattle right on the edge of what is now the Timbavati Reserve. He used to take them all over the place to graze, accompanying them on horseback, Wild West style. He was fond of boasting that in his first year down here he notched up eighty lions, including one that he shot while sitting at dinner.

He was in the middle of his meal when he spotted a pair of eyes outside the rondavel. From their height and distance apart, he knew they were the eyes of a lion. He called out to his wife who was in the kitchen and asked her to bring him his gun and a flashlight. She did so, but Jan didn't use the light. He simply shot at the eyes from where he was sitting and killed the lion stone dead – without even bothering to stand up.

Jan had an ox that he had hand-reared from birth, and he was very fond of this animal. One night a lion got into his camp and killed the ox. Jan immediately took his rifle and a flashlight and went out and lay down beside the carcass of the ox, knowing that the lion would return for the meat. When the lion appeared he waited until it approached within five yards, then killed it with his first shot.

There was another farmer, we'll call him Moss, in the Timbavati district around this time. He went out one night after a party and, full of drink, he was determined to shoot a lion he'd heard roaring outside his camp. He had a gun bearer with him and it was a very wet night. When his vehicle got bogged down in the mud, Moss decided to leave it there and go after his lion on foot, using his flashlight. After they had walked for a bit, he picked up a pair of eyes in the beam of his light. He took aim and fired, dead between the eyes. Nothing happened: the eyes remained there looking back at him, unblinkingly. Moss was a very good shot and used to pride himself on the fact that he never missed. He couldn't understand what had happened. He fired again. Still the eyes remained there, staring back at him. Then his gun bearer tapped him on the shoulder. Moss looked up, saw his amused expression and suddenly understood. He walked forward, straight toward the still glowing eyes, and found that he hadn't missed after all. There were two bullet holes clean through the radiator of his jeep.

On another occasion Moss went out after some lions with a party of eight, including his wife and Gustav Battenhausen, who told me about it. Moss spotted a lion in the beam of his flashlight and fired. They paced the distance out later; it was less than twenty yards away.

The lion sank down, then started to rise again, growling ferociously.

Moss started to walk toward it, and as there's nothing in the world more dangerous than a wounded lion, two members of the party fired shots into the animal to make sure that it was dead. Moss turned to them with his back to the lion, which was still growling horribly, and shouted: "Stop firing into my bloody lion. Stop making holes in my lion skin." Then, when he got quite close to the dying animal, he crouched down, shining his light into the bush. "This is the best bait we're ever likely to get," he said. After a few moments, a lioness came out of the bush, attracted by the roars of the dying lion. Moss put two shots into her. She ran off, then fell about fifty or sixty paces away, still very much alive. Moss stood up and started to walk toward the lioness, shouting over his shoulder: "Don't shoot at me, you bloody fools." He walked right up to the lioness and shot her dead at point-blank range. He then went back and killed his "bait" with a shot through the head, saying, "Well, I think that will do us for one evening."

They were tough in those days, and they had their own very strict rules of conduct. An unforgivable crime was to leave a lion wounded in the bush. If you wounded a lion, it was your responsibility to finish it off there and then. There was no way you could evade that responsibility.

A man who was doing some surveying near Timbavati was invited by friends to go on a lion hunt in the Timbavati region. He went out with them and they wounded two lionesses in a pride. As it happened, he wounded the first and one of the friends wounded the second. The two wounded lionesses ran away down a dry riverbed and hid among some reeds.

"What do we do now?" he asked.

His friends handed him a revolver, a big Colt. "All right, go ahead," they said. "We'll be right behind you."

"Must I go in there? I know nothing about lions."

"You wounded the lion," said one of the friends. "So you go ahead now and finish her off. If you turn back, we shoot you."

203

He carefully followed the blood spoor through the reeds and eventually came to where the lioness was lying, drowsy from her wounds, and finished her off. "Right," his friend said. "You did very well there. Now let's go after the other lion."

But he had had enough. He handed them back the Colt and said: "This other one wasn't even mine. I'm done with hunting. You can even keep my skin, for all I care."

Battenhausen also told me about a man we'll call Hans, who was managing a large cattle ranch just outside Timbavati. Hans didn't much like the isolated life down there so "he got himself married," as Battenhausen put it, and brought his young wife down to live in the camp with him. During the honeymoon Hans went out after the lions one night, shooting two inside his cattle compound and wounding a third, a lioness. He was tracking the animal down, to kill her off, and the blood spoor happened to take him right past his own camp.

His wife came out and joined them. Hans warned her it was a very dangerous business, and told her to stay well behind. Unfortunately, they walked right past the wounded lioness. She charged and Hans's wife, being last in line, was knocked down.

Hans shot the lioness, right there as it crouched on top of the woman. Then he pulled the lioness off her and asked if she was all right. There wasn't a mark on her, not even a bruise, but she said that she felt very strange. Hans took her straight to the hospital, where they discovered that her liver had been completely smashed with one blow from the lioness. "I'm sorry," the doctor said, "but there's no way we can replace the liver." The woman died that night.

A neighbor of Battenhausen's who had a luxury camp,

fully fenced in and equipped with a swimming pool, was there with his wife and a new servant. In the morning the servant got up, lit her lantern and went into the kitchen to make coffee, followed, as she thought, by the camp dog. A few minutes later the woman came bursting into the main rondavel saying that she had been in the kitchen with the dog when suddenly a lion walked in.

Having calmed her down a bit, the wife then explained that they didn't happen to have a dog. They went back to the kitchen and found that there were indeed *two* lions there. Not only that, but there were fifteen lions in all inside the enclosure, prowling around and drinking out of the swimming pool. Battenhausen's friend got the jeep, rounded them up and forced them back out through a hole in the enclosure which had been made by elephants.

There is really no kind of fencing that will keep lions out. If the elephants make a hole, the lions will certainly make use of it, because they always take the easiest course. But if there's no break in a fence and they want to get in or out, they'll go right over the top or crawl underneath. Battenhausen himself has watched a full-grown lion launch itself again and again at a high stockade, constructed of nine-inch-wide trees right up against one another, about twelve feet high and reinforced with thick thorn branches. It was an eerie sight, he said, to see this huge lion, obviously in great pain, hurling itself again and again at the prickly fence without uttering a murmur of complaint. It emphasized for him just how strong these animals are. I myself have seen lions scrambling under the "game-proof" fencing of the Kruger National Park. It doesn't even seem to slow them down.

These stories of thirty years ago point up two things: the changing attitude of man toward the idea of killing lions and the fact that lions are basically extremely dangerous – and completely unpredictable. There is an African woman called Mrs. Marula living in the area now, and she has been known to chase lions off a kill simply because she wanted the meat for herself. There are times when a pack of hyenas can chase a pride of lions off a kill. There are other times when a lioness will claw a vulture out of the sky, leaping five or six feet into the air to do so, simply because the vulture is irritating her. People who live with lions all their lives – zoo curators, for example – always emphasize this utter unpredictability, even in captivity: it is the lion you trust most that is likely to lash out one day and gash your arm.

If you spend months on end watching the lions in the wild, as I have done, it is very easy to take them for granted and allow your interest in their behavior patterns and their apparent disinterest in jeeps to obscure your fear of them. But it's a great mistake. Lions are not only terribly powerful but totally ruthless.

Schaller makes the interesting point that there is an evolutionary explanation for the extremely high mortality rate of lion cubs. Lions live for a relatively long time, sixteen or seventeen years on average, and are so immensely strong that they have no natural enemies apart from man. Of all the animals that inhabit the bush, elephants and lions are eaten almost exclusively as carrion. Nothing can or will attempt to attack them in their prime. Therefore, lions cannot afford to raise indiscriminate numbers of young. If they did, they would be in danger of wiping out their own source of food. In general, in the wild, you sometimes find lionesses abandoning their litters or losing some of their cubs, which are immediately brought down by hyenas. You also find male lions lying on the cubs and crushing them to death, or fatally injuring them when driving them off a kill. You even find cannabalism, though on an extremely small scale.

One afternoon, a few weeks after I had shot the Musketeer, I was surprised to find that the pride had been joined by a strange young male, a few months older than the two remaining Musketeers and Suzie Wong. I imagine that he had recently been thrown out by an adjoining pride, probably one from the Kruger National Park, and had happened to come upon my pride and to fit into the niche that I recently – and regretfully – created.

For three or four weeks I saw him with the others regularly; then, just as abruptly as he had appeared, he disappeared. I can only surmise what happened: the two pride males initially accepted him, taking him for granted as the missing Musketeer, and then suddenly stumbled onto the fact that he was a young lion from a strange pride and threw him out.

The fact that he had been thrown out by his own pride at this particular stage of his life indicates pretty clearly that the other two Musketeers haven't all that much time left. They will probably have to leave the pride within four to six months. Suzie Wong seems to have been completely accepted by the pride and will probably stay on as one of the pride lionesses. Then, within another year or less, it may be Temba and Vela's turn to go.

If they do have to leave the pride, the young lions will initially become nomads, hunting either as a pair or singly, until (or if) they find a pride which they can take over. There is the slim chance, however, that they might challenge

Achilles and Agamemnon and oust them from their positions of authority.

If that did occur, or if a pair of nomads from another pride happened to come in and take over the Machaton pride, which is even more likely, Achilles and Agamemnon would be forced to return to their nomadic existence. They would probably hunt initially as a pair, until one or the other of them became too weak to hunt effectively. The weak one would then be deserted by his companion and would almost certainly be brought down by hyenas.

The end of a pride male is almost always a sad and solitary affair. A thorn in the foot, or any leg injury which prevents him from stalking effectively, or an illness of any kind, even sheer exhaustion, and he is immediately at the mercy of the scavengers he once despised. A couple of hyenas can easily bring him down.

CHAPTER TWELVE

Phuma and the Wayward Gene

WHEN I FINISHED MY TERM as temporary game warden and the current warden, Trygve Cooper, took over, Pierre Hugo, my father's neighbor at Vlak, approached me with the idea of turning one of his two camps into a game-viewing lodge for small parties of tourists. He asked Charlotte and me to take it over and look after the conversion. This arrangement suited me fine because it enabled us to stay in the area and keep an eye on our lions.

The new camp was to be called Tanda-tula. Unfortunately, between supervising the complete modernization of the rondavels and the installation of an electric-generating plant and a completely new plumbing system, we were kept extremely busy and I found that I had very little time to spend with the lions. But I knew they were there, within a half hour's drive, and at least I could see them from time to time.

During this period, Charlotte did a brief stint as a cook

on safari in Botswana. Pierre Hugo had heard that a safari tour company was looking for a cook for several trips and thought that this would give Charlotte a good idea of how other camps were run.

As it turned out conditions on the safari couldn't have been more different from those at Tanda-tula. The trek in each case was ten days into the wild and ten days back. On the first trip they had only ten guests, and on the second twenty. There were Germans, Swiss, French and South Africans. Charlotte said that the twenty-guest trip was absolutely incredible. She's never seen so much booze in her life in any one place. Every evening was like New Year's Eve.

She slept out in the open most of the time and it was really highly dangerous, because in the Botswana safari trade no one is allowed to carry firearms, not even for self-defense or shooting for rations. The guides and drivers and cooks really have to be quite brave and resourceful to operate under those conditions, as the country is infested with elephants, lions, rhinos, hyenas and other extremely dangerous animals.

In the meantime I was working away at Tanda-tula and slipping out to look at the lions whenever I could find the time.

As early as May, some eight months after we found the white cubs, I discovered that Scarleg had two new cubs. I had caught a glimpse of them right at the edge of the thick riverine bush. Suzie Wong, who appeared to be acting in the capacity of nursemaid, seemed to be leading them out to me; but it could have been that she was leading them away from a kill, for their own safety. They were normal, tawny cubs, and very small – no bigger than large rabbits. I saw only two, but I sensed that there were almost certainly others around.

Then, in August, while driving a pickup truck near Piggy Dam, I spotted the spoor of several lionesses and cubs leading across the river. There were a lot of tracks. In the back of the truck were my two friends: Andrew Williamson, a lawyer, and John Dunning, warden of the nearby Giraffe Private Nature Reserve. In the cab with me was Andrew's wife, Jill. Charlotte was still on safari in Botswana, and Tabs was in Johannesburg staying with my sister Lan.

We crossed the river and suddenly we came upon the lions. At first we saw the three lionesses and four cubs, but it soon became clear that there were more about. Finally they all emerged from the bush and came down the river bank toward us. There were four lionesses and about ten cubs, though at first we couldn't count the cubs or even see them very clearly because they were all bunched together and tripping under the feet of the lionesses. The fact that there were so many cubs came as a complete surprise to me. After seeing Scarleg's two cubs with Suzie Wong back in May, I had suspected there must be more, but certainly not this many. In their infancy the cubs had obviously been kept well hidden in the thick riverine bush.

The group ran off along the river bank and we followed them. The lionesses were very alert and wary.

They stopped under a shingayi tree and Andrew suddenly said excitedly, "There's one of the white ones."

I couldn't see either Temba or Tombi in the group and I was a bit doubtful that either of them was there because I couldn't see any sign of Tabby. I knew also that this was the wrong subgroup.

After a few minutes the cubs began to move out, one by one, from under the shade of the shingayi and straight toward the truck. The sixth cub to emerge was white, and only about six weeks old – every bit as white as Temba and Tombi had been at that age.

We called the new cub Phuma (pronounced Póo-ma) from the Zulu for "to stand out" or "to be out of the ordinary."

It was difficult to tell Phuma's sex that day as the cubs were tripping and falling over each other, and it was impossible to isolate Phuma in the binoculars. But after observing them a few more times, we knew that she was female.

I've always had some difficulty in telling all the lionesses apart, and this day – special as it was – was no different. Golden, Scarleg and Suzie Wong were there, certainly, but the fourth lioness had me puzzled. It could have been either Greta or Lona, one of the two that we seldom saw with the pride, but I just couldn't be certain.

But there was something puzzling me far more than the identity of the lionesses. Which of them, I wondered, had given birth to the new white cub?

Of course, I knew that there was no way of telling. There never is, in the wild, because cubs will suckle indiscriminately on any lactating lioness. I have had to resign myself to the fact that this is something we are never going to know.

There was one mystery, however, that was now one step nearer to being solved, a mystery that had baffled me ever since the day we first discovered the white cubs.

There was no doubt about Temba and Tombi's parentage. Joe Zamboni and I had actually seen Agamemnon and Tabby mating. The question remained, though: which of them was carrying the wayward gene?

As Tabby was not with this subgroup and as it is extremely unusual for a lion to mate with a pride lioness while she is still rearing her cubs, I could be reasonably certain that Tabby was not Phuma's mother.

So the wayward gene must have come from the father – Agamemnon. This raises the intriguing possibility that more white cubs may be born to the Machaton pride. I also realized that, as a result of inbreeding, it was quite possible that the white strain exists not only in Agamemnon, but in one or more of the pride lionesses as well – and even possibly, if they are twin brothers, in Achilles.

Phuma, like Temba and Tombi, is a normal lion in every respect – except for her color.

Once I recovered from the shock of finding another white cub, I studied the remaining nine in closer detail. What was particularly interesting about this new crop of cubs was that there seemed to be a distinct gradation of color from the pure white of Phuma, through various paler, blond shades, to the normal tawny gold of Vela and the Musketeers.

We saw the cubs several times that August. I was again very worried about all the dangers that threatened Phuma. The chances of all ten surviving was very slight; and by the law of averages, it seemed highly unlikely that Phuma would be one of the survivors.

On the other hand, four lionesses make a formidable hunting pack and the new cubs were being extremely well provided for. On several occasions we saw them on giraffe kills, where the victims had been in the prime of life. These were not giraffe that had been caught drinking at a waterhole, when they stretch their forelegs out wide to reach the water and are therefore highly vulnerable to attack. They were giraffe that had been simply attacked on the Plains and brought down.

Shortly after Charlotte returned from safari, she, Tabs and I, and two of our friends spent the entire day watching the lionesses and their new cubs on a giraffe kill. All five of us were piled into a tiny Honda motorcar.

At first nothing much happened. A few cubs ate, but mostly they just lay around panting under the shade of a shingayi. There were two jackals skirting around the area trotting in to try and snatch at the meat and then trit-trotting away again as soon as Scarleg threatened them. One of them just wouldn't learn. As soon as he'd been chased off the kill, he came trit-trotting back to try it from another angle, only to be threatened again. It was quite hilarious – like watching a Tom and Jerry cartoon.

Then in the afternoon it started to rain. The whole plain suddenly seemed to be full of lions – four full-grown lionesses and ten cubs frolicking all over the plain. The little ones were soon covered in mud. They love romping in the mud and rain.

They played all the usual games that we'd watched Temba, Tombi and Vela at: Pig in the Middle, Tug of War (with the dead giraffe's tail), Stalk a Tail, as well as familiar routines like jumping on top of each other and getting up on their hind legs and clawing at each other. And all the time this trit-trotting jackal kept at it, still trying to nip in and grab a bit of the giraffe carcass.

We spent the whole day there. Then, just before dark, three rhinos appeared, snuffling right up to the lions. The cubs immediately stalked them, using trees and shrubs as cover – just as Temba, Tombi and Vela had done in their earlier days.

Eventually the rhinos were within six paces of our tiny Honda and were milling around between us and the lions. They were clearly very nervous and jumpy. They were anxious both about the lions and about the car. We weren't feeling all that comfortable either, because if the rhinos had taken fright and bolted in our direction they would have flattened the tiny Honda. They're huge animals and they were towering over it.

After what seemed like ages, they lumbered off in the opposite direction and we went on watching the lions. They stayed on that kill for three days, keeping the vultures and jackals off until the entire carcass was utterly demolished.

Normally lions eat only about 70 percent of a kill; the remainder is left for the hyenas, jackals, vultures and other scavengers. It is interesting to note that the sharp distinction which used to be drawn between scavengers and predators is now far less rigid. Lions will eat carrion; I've seen them eating meat that was crawling with maggots. Hyenas are basically scavengers, but they also do some killing. Probably the only pure scavengers – if pure is a word you can use for them – are vultures.

Because I was busy working at Tanda-tula, I wasn't able to watch Phuma's development as closely as I had watched Temba and Tombi. In fact, I've only seen Phuma about thirty times so far, but already she seems to have far more spirit than the other two. We've observed her tripping up one of the Musketeers on one of the rare occasions when the two subgroups were together. She walked straight up to this

Musketeer, slapped his leg and made him trip. She's extremely aggressive on a kill, chasing all the other cubs off until she's had her fill, and she's very cocky toward our vehicles. She's the one that always comes closest.

By now it was September and as they approached their first birthday, Tabby's cubs were also thriving. Seen in silhouette alongside Tombi, Temba's body seems heavier, his chest deeper, his jaw fuller. Tombi is sleeker, her face sharper, her coat slightly whiter. Vela was rapidly losing the darker spots of a normal baby lion. The three are clearly still pals. Following their fortunes, I've seen minor friction, never a serious clash.

I saw them again just before the rains came. I was out looking for them and spotted four vultures sitting on a tree, a sure sign of a kill. It could have been anywhere within a four-hundred-yard radius of where the vultures were, because the scavengers tend to keep at a respectable distance. It was a bit like looking for a needle in a haystack, but nevertheless we parked the car, waited, and eventually heard a lot of growling and snapping. We found them on a wildebeest kill — the two Musketeers, Dimples, and Tabby and her three cubs, all as fat as butter and in prime condition.

By this time, even Phuma, at four and a half months, was past the first perilous period of a lion cub's life.

So, despite my earlier concern, it looks as if there is a chance that, with help, the white lions of Timbavati will survive.

CHAPTER THIRTEEN

To Those Who Come After

BY NOW I HAD SPENT TWO years in the Lowveld living with the lions, and I found myself deeply involved in two issues. One was the future of Timbavati, the place itself, as one bit of the wild that has survived unchanged for millions of years. The other was the future of my white lions.

The more I learn about Timbavati, the more it seems to me that it should be preserved exactly as it is. All around us this ancient area of Africa is slowly being eaten into by civilization. But here, there has been no interruption in the pattern of evolution since long before the dawn of our species.

In this part of the world, almost five and a half million years ago, *Australopithecus* evolved, a discovery made by Raymond Dart about a hundred miles north of Timbavati. They were probably only about five feet tall and weighed no more than 130 pounds, but they walked erect and could use their hands to construct simple tools and weapons.

About a million years ago *Australopithecus* was succeeded by *Homo erectus*, one of the first varieties of true man who used the brain he had to discover the potential of fire and began to change the world in which he found himself. Thus this whole area of Africa must be regarded as one of the very cradles of the human race. It is also one of the few areas where modern man has intervened without destroying all the wild creatures around him.

As the motto of the Timbavati Reserve states, this wildlife is not ours to dispose of as we please. We must account for it to those who come after.

I only hope that the ever more pressing demands of Africa's human population will not result in the place being given over to some form of "progress." It would be tragic if mere expediency resulted in the obliteration of what were among man's first footprints on this earth. Even more important, we must try to preserve what remains of the environment that existed in perfect stability before his arrival, and before the subsequent arrival of language, thought, invention and ultimately civilization and industrialization upset the working of the entire ecosystem.

My other, and even more urgent concern was the future of the white lions.

From an evolutionary point of view, it might be said that the white lions are largely a curiosity. There are now white tigers in zoos in Delhi, Bristol and Washington, all bred from one white male tiger who was found in the wild, and was mated with his granddaughter and in turn with her offspring. The propagation of these white tigers has been a man-made situation. Theoretically, this would never occur

218

in the wild on any long-term basis because it is not an advantage for a tiger – or a lion, for that matter – to be white.

On the other hand, the fact that there is a steady gradation from tawny to white among the Machaton pride seems to indicate that there is a gene here that tends to work toward a white strain.

The white lions are beautiful. They were irresistible as cubs, and I am eager to find a way to ensure the survival of the strain.

Natural selection usually prevents brother and sister lions from mating with each other in the wild. So it is unlikely that Temba and Tombi would ever mate naturally, even if they were thrown out of the pride together. It could be stage-managed, of course, by putting them together in some sort of enclosure. But once you place them in such an artificial environment, there would be very little chance that they would ever be accepted back into the pride.

I've often wondered whether the best idea wouldn't be to hedge our bets and send the white male, Temba, off to a zoo now: quickly, before he is thrown out of the pride and exposed to the dangers outside the protection of the reserve; and while he is still young enough to settle down in a zoo. If we did that, it would provide revenue for the reserve for use in its wildlife management program. The funds could also be used to purchase electronic tracking and monitoring equipment to enable us to keep in constant touch with Tombi and Phuma.

In this way we would have the best of two worlds. Breeding experiments could be carried out with Temba in a zoo, under controlled conditions. And, at the same time, we would still have two white lions in the wild to continue to study.

If Tombi is not thrown out by the pride, there would be a strong possibility of her mating with Agamemnon, and there might well be further white cubs. In the meantime Phuma would also be growing up in the wild, and we would have another chance because she too might mate with Agamemnon, or even with some other pride male – possibly Vela – who could well carry the white gene.

In this way we would at least be doing everything in our power to ensure that this is not the end, but only the beginning of the story of the white lions of Timbavati.